ABOUT THE AUTHOR

Dr. Talley, a professor in the Department of Psychiatry and Behavioral Sciences of Duke University Medical Center and a psychologist and an associate director at Counseling and Psychological Services of Duke University, has been practicing, teaching, supervising, and conducting research in the area of brief and very brief psychotherapy for over thirty-five years. He has published seven books on this and related topics and is a Fellow of The American Psychological Association, The American Academy of Clinical Psychology, and The American Academy of Counseling Psychology of which he is also President Emeritus. He has been a frequent Board Certification Examiner for The American Board of Professional Psychology and is Chair and Chief Executive Officer Emeritus of the Council of Presidents of Psychology Specialty Academies.

A special thanks to Amanda Potter for her final formatting and contributing the cover photograph.

FOREWORD

As Joseph E. Talley points out in his "Practicing Notes and Tools..." the reality today is that brief therapy is psychotherapy in this country. Accordingly, there are a plethora of books on the subject, including many on brief dynamic therapy. But to my knowledge, Talley's "Notes" are the only summary of basic principles and techniques in cliff notes form. However, it is more than this. The author provides some of the best concrete illustrations of focal case formulations that I have seen. He also suggests some very creative, specific methods for introducing transference interpretations into your work when conducting brief dynamic treatment. This issue is particularly important since there is solid empirical evidence that in this form of treatment transference interpretations are risky and must be used judiciously. By the way, this is an example of how Talley rests his discussions on relevant empirical findings. His discussion of the use of metaphors and fairy tales is fascinating. The most unique part of the "Notes" is the author's discussion of evoking and using emotions through the "affect bridge" technique, as well as his suggestions for integrating Ericksonian (i.e., Milton Erickson), gestalt, and solution focused techniques into a brief dynamic approach. He takes a truly integrative perspective. I enthusiastically recommend these "Notes" to practicing therapists of all degrees of experience.

Jeffrey L. Binder, Ph.D., ABPP
Georgia School of Professional Psychology
Atlanta, Georgia

TABLE OF CONTENTS

1. Brief Integrative Psychodynamic Psychotherapy — 1

2. Why Brief Psychotherapy? — 6

3. Historical and Research Notes — 8

4. Major Differences Between Brief, Very Brief, Open-Ended (Longer-Term) and Crisis Intervention Psychotherapy — 11

5. Considerations Concerning Who Is Most Likely to Benefit from Brief Integrative Psychodynamic Treatment — 17

6. Therapist Selection Criteria: Who Can Do Brief Psychotherapy Better? — 23

7. The Underlying, Overarching Macro-Technique: General Treatment Interventions of the Therapist — 28

8. Specific Micro-Techniques Useable in Brief Psychotherapy — 33

9. Assessment and Evaluation: The Initial Sessions — 36

10. The Therapeutic Alliance — 42

11. Establishing the Focus — 48

12. Some Standard Core Conflictual Relationship Theme (CCRT) Categories	58
13. Some Thoughts on Transference, Immediacy and "Here and Now" Work in the Relationship	60
14. Affect Bridge Technique	66
15. Metaphors of the Problem	72
16. Therapeutic Stories and Tales	77
17. Opposite Feeling Affect Bridge Variation	84
18. Some Contributions of Milton Erickson Regarding Therapeutic Communication	87
19. Micro-Technique of the Problem Solving Daydream and Active Imagination	92
20. Active Imagination and the Inner Guide	96
21. Contrasting Videos: A Variation of the Miracle Question	100
22. Therapist Wordings of Comments and Responses	103
23. Thoughts on the Brief Treatment of Grief	110
24. Closing and Ending in Brief Therapy	113
References	115

1.

Brief Integrative Psychodynamic Psychotherapy

What is brief? Most all psychotherapy is now brief except in training clinics or among the introspective, well-to-do, out-of-pocket payment private practices. Many findings from surveys including NIMH data have found that the mean number of outpatient sessions attended by a person is less than five sessions in public clinics (Garfield, 1994). Even including private practices, Olfson and Pincus (1994) found that seventy percent of all outpatients in the United States were seen for ten or fewer sessions. So actually, most psychotherapy has been brief, but by default and not by design. For additional supporting data see Levenson (2010). Even good health insurance benefits often will pay only for up to approximately 26 sessions (six months of weekly sessions) per year.

Most importantly the classic studies that show that psychotherapy itself is effective, really show that brief psychotherapy is effective because the mean number of sessions in the studies was less than 26 sessions. For example, in the historic Smith, Glass, and Miller (1980) meta-analytic study often cited as the proof that psychotherapy works, the average number of sessions in the studies was 17. The studies by Howard, Kopta, Krause, and Orlinsky (1986) and Howard, Moras, Brill, Martinovich, and Lutz (1996) show that the greatest incremental progress happened during the first eight sessions. Likewise, the multi-site, NIMH study (Elkin, Shea, Watkins, Imber, Sotsky, Collins, et al. (1989) showing the efficacy of cognitive-behavioral therapy (CBT) and interpersonal therapy (IPT) in the treatment of depression had a mean number of 16 sessions.

It is true that the studies by Howard and colleagues (1986 & 1996) show that improvements continued for up to two years during weekly sessions. Yet, 75% of all patients in the studies showed measurable improvement in the first six months of weekly sessions. Other more recent studies have also shown that significant symptom improvement can occur in brief psychotherapy (Talley & Clack, 2006) and in very brief psychotherapy lasting less than seven sessions as well (Talley, Butcher, Maguire, & Pinkerton, 1992). Yet, consumer satisfaction with psychotherapy has been shown to be greater when the psychotherapy lasted for up to two years of weekly sessions (Seligman, 1995).

Historically, brief has usually been defined as between eight and 25 sessions, or two to six months of weekly work, (Koss & Shiang, 1994) although the renowned author of psychotherapy texts, Lewis Wolberg, is said to have maintained that any therapy lasting less than a year is brief. Having from one to seven sessions, if not designed as crisis intervention, has been called very brief psychotherapy, ultra-brief psychotherapy or a very brief intervention. We even have single session psychotherapy (Talmon, 1990).

Freud's earliest cases were brief including one lasting for four hours on a hike and others lasting several sessions. What then, caused psychotherapy to lengthen? First, Freud was initially using psychoanalysis as a tool to understand the personality and the workings of the mind making the rapidity of psychotherapy of no necessary value. Then, when he was attempting to cure ills, he discovered and began to focus on the transference which required the analyst to be less active and directive and that also slowed the process down. Additionally, the analyst became more passive with the yielding of hypnosis and suggestion to free association. Finally, a therapeutic perfectionism likewise developed in which no stone was to be left unturned, increasing the emphasis on past history instead of emphasizing the present problem which in turn also served to lengthen treatment. We can see from Freud's early work that therapy could be brief as a function of time expectations, but also as a function of the goals and methods of therapy (Levenson, 2010).

The treatment described here is integrative because it is open to utilizing most techniques from most schools of psychotherapy. It could be called technically eclectic but not simply eclectic or theoretically eclectic because although the macro-technique integrates elements of cognitive and behavioral (CBT) techniques, affective or emotion focused (EFT) techniques, and social or interpersonal (IPT) techniques as well as psychodynamic and gestalt techniques; it rests on relational, developmental, and psychodynamic theory. The approach is designed to improve the functioning of the psyche and therefore the well-being of the person whether they are seen as a patient needing remediation or alleviation of an illness, seen as a client wanting to improve well-being in living, or seen as a seeker wanting growth.

It is called psychotherapy because a process that addresses how one sees the world and themselves in relation to it while considering all in their thoughts and feelings and experiences that have been, currently are, and that they can imagine ever to be, warrants a word for something large, broad, and deep.

It is a quest to help one become as fully functioning and feeling of well-being as is possible. It is designed to improve the functioning of the psyche and it is an effort to re-tool and shape the elements of being that might receive counseling about a situation in life. It is about traits of being and the elements of being that govern those traits such as motives, strivings, and inhibitions, wishes, and fears. It might be about the management of emotions, about addressing their origins, their effects, and modifying how the processes operate to improve the person's on-going emotional functioning, or about thoughts, beliefs, values, and choices. Psychotherapy may look at the themes of thought, their possible motives, goals, and assumptions, or even the utility and value of the effects of these thoughts on the rest of one's being, behavior, and others.

What is this treatment for? Since all psychotherapy treatment studies are by and large done on brief treatment, identified as such or not, the fitting of the treatment to the problem is really the issue. Anxiety, depression, anger, and problems with interpersonal relationships are all workable in brief treatment as is grief work and problem clarification. Likewise the problems that challenge psychotherapy in general are more difficult in brief psychotherapy such as problems with addiction or impulse control.

If the treatment is modified to fit the problem, the question becomes one of what is the best tailoring and adaptation of the treatment to fit the problem and the person. Whether or not brief therapy is advised has more to do with the severity of the problem, the person's motivation for change, and the person's other capacities rather than the specific presenting problem itself.

© J.E. Talley, Ph.D.

2.

Why Brief Psychotherapy?
It's not just economics.

- A growing realization that usual length therapy did not meet the needs of many (e.g., addictions, conduct disorders and those not psychology minded).

- People and especially the less educated and males did not stay in long-term therapy. (the majority attended less than 20 times and the NIMH median has been approximately 4.7 sessions).

- Long ago Garfield (1994) found that 66% of patients concluded therapy by the 6th session and only 10% continued through 25 sessions.

- Talley (1992) found that of Duke University young adults seeking services 80% - 90% attended less than 8 sessions though they could attend at least 16 and no co-pay was charged.

SO FOR MANY YEARS WE HAVE BEEN PRACTICING BRIEF THERAPY, BUT BY DEFAULT AND NOT BY DESIGN.

- Freud's original work was brief but grew in length with transference, the analyst's passivity with free association, and a historical focus contributing to therapeutic perfectionism.

- The *personalities of therapists* may also have led to their work being more interactive and therefore briefer (e.g., Rank, Alexander and French, Ferenzi, etc.).

- The *de-idealization of long-term psychotherapy* - no personality transplants have yet been documented.

- Efficiency and "more" in less time is a beacon in all scientific searches.

- Curiosity is always a strong motive for experimentation.

Research Supports its Efficacy

The literature that demonstrates that psychotherapy is effective actually concludes that *brief* psychotherapy is effective because the average number of sessions in the studies is less than 26 (e.g., Smith, Glass, & Miller, 1980; Elkin et al., 1989). Psychotherapy as it is now practiced except in training clinics and out-of-pocket fee clinics is of the length that had been called brief psychotherapy. Psychotherapy now *is* brief psychotherapy.

- Smith, Glass, and Miller (1980) conclude that "psychotherapy is effective" with a meta-analysis with 475 studies but the mean number of sessions was 17.

- Even as far back as 1984, Horowitz, Marmor, Krupnick, and their colleagues found that brief treatment is effective with "fairly severe" psychiatric symptoms in reducing and maintaining lower symptoms.

- Howard, Kopta, Krause, and Orlinsky (1986) and Howard, Moras, Brill, Martinovich, and Lutz (1996) on "The Dose Effect Relation in Psychotherapy".
    — By 8 sessions 50% of all patients are "measurably improved" and 75% by 26 sessions.
    — A meta-analysis with over 2,400 patients.
    — There was a diagnosis differential influencing response.

- NIMH treatment of depression study, CBT and IPT treatment (for 16 sessions) with medication was most effective (Elkin et al., 1989).

- Talley, Butcher, Maguire, and Pinkerton (1992) in a Duke CAPS study of very brief therapy – recipients were "quite satisfied" and symptoms were down significantly. Talley and Clack (2006) also showed significant symptom improvement with brief therapy.

- BUT - ALAS! *Consumer Reports* (Seligman, 1995) found that people in treatment for 2 years were more satisfied.

© J.E. Talley, Ph.D.

3.

Historical and Research Notes

1. Psychotherapy was originally intended to be brief. Freud's first cases were brief and very brief with some lasting between one and four hours.

2. Analysis lengthened because:

    a. It was a research tool to understand personality and psychological phenomena in general;

    b. The concept of transference and the need to "work through" it developing;

    c. The concept of the multi-determination of symptoms and the need to uncover and work through each antecedent which led to "therapeutic perfectionism";

    d. The use of free association replacing hypnosis and suggestion.

3. Rank, Alexander and French, and others later (Ferenczi, Wolberg, Malan, Davanloo, Sifneos, Strupp and Binder, and Mann) attempted to shorten it again, in part to be efficient and innovative and probably to suit their personalities.

4. On the other hand, a congressional investigation of mental health services in the U.S. in the late 1950's led to the establishment of community mental health centers in the 1960's because:

    a. The usual lengthy treatment didn't benefit many including those with addictions, conduct problems and "those not psychologically minded";

    b. NIMH data showed repeatedly that people attended an average of about 4.7 sessions and then didn't return.

5. a. Garfield (1994) found that two thirds of all clients terminated by the sixth session.

    b. Talley, Butcher, Maguire, and Pinkerton (1992) showed for those attending for one to seven sessions a mean rating of "quite satisfied" with the services received (7 on a scale of 1-10) and statistically significant symptom decreases.

    c. In a meta-analysis of over 2,400 outpatients Howard, Kopta, Krause, and Orlinsky (1986) found that by the eighth session 53% of depressed patients, 46% of anxious patients, and even 33% of borderline and psychotic patients rated themselves as improved.

So there's been movement toward brief and very brief treatment apart from the economic pressures to do so.

6. Research reported in *The Heart and Soul of Change* (Hubble, Duncan, & Miller, 1999) and by Larry Beutler (2000), suggests that building client expectation, hope, and sense of "self-efficacy" (that they can be of help to themselves) are probably more primary ingredients for positive outcome than technique with many to most problems. The item on the client satisfaction

scale in the study by Talley, Butcher, and Moorman (1992) that best predicted client satisfaction was, "The counselor encouraged me to believe I could improve the situation."

© J.E. Talley, Ph.D.

4.

Major Differences Between Brief, Very Brief, Open-Ended (Longer-Term) and Crisis Intervention Psychotherapy

Historically, brief psychotherapy has been defined as differing from open-ended and very brief psychotherapy as well as crisis intervention not only in length or duration, but also with regard to the goals usually thought to be accomplished by its practice, the methods it employs, and the indications for its use (Aguilera & Messick, 1978; Marmor, 1979; Talley, 1992; Pinkerton, Talley, & Cooper, 2009).

Duration

Crisis intervention and very brief psychotherapy are most often described as lasting from one through seven sessions while brief psychotherapy is usually characterized as lasting from eight to twenty-six sessions or, said differently, from two to six months of weekly treatment. Open-ended psychotherapy might be thought of as anything lasting longer than that, however, long-term treatment has often been described as lasting one or more years.

Goals

The goals of brief and very brief psychotherapy typically are to resolve a core conflict, to improve adaptive coping capacities, or to decrease or remove symptoms. By contrast, the goal of crisis intervention is usually described as the need to re-establish equilibrium with a secondary goal at times being to remove a symptom and/or to improve coping. The goal of open-ended or long-term treatment has been described as personality reconstruction. However, it is questionable how much, if any, actual reconstruction of the personality can occur and the data to support its occurrence has not been as forthcoming as had been expected. This leaves the goals for open-ended (longer-term) psychotherapy being to treat those with greater symptom severity, lower motivation, more time needed to develop the alliance, or the presence of more entrenched habits of personality than can be ameliorated in brief psychotherapy.

Additional goals for brief or very brief psychotherapy include the following:

1. A new and more useful understanding of the problem;

2. A new and more useful understanding of personal strengths and internal resources to bring to bear or use with the problem;

3. A new understanding of external resources available for use to help with the problem;

4. A new understanding of skills one can learn, practice, and develop for greater mastery with the problem;

5. A new plan, strategy, or set of tasks to use for greater mastery with the problem;

6. Gain a sense of acceptance perhaps after a catharsis of sorts;

7. Gain a sense of "permission" that it's understandable ("okay") to think, act, or feel in a particular way;

8. Gain a sense of hope about the future and being or becoming able in one way or another to successfully meet life's challenges;

9. To provide psychoeducation.

Methods

The methods of brief psychotherapy might be described as follows:

A focus on the present with the exploration of the past conflicts only as they relate to the present core conflict;

A directed focus on the core conflict;

Establishing and utilizing a positive transference and the exploration of this transference much more cautiously, in a less interpretive and more wondering aloud mode;

A balanced emphasis tailored to the individual on support along with confrontation, interpretation, exploration, and explanation;

Active participation in focusing on the core conflict and related wondering, interpretation, confrontation, and observation;

The rare use of environmental management;

Usually employing a more integrative or eclectic approach.

Crisis intervention utilizes the methods of:

Focusing on the precipitating event and linking this to the past only for a historical review of previous crises and their management if relevant and applicable to the present crisis;

A directed focus on the crisis and on an emotional abreaction of pent-up feelings attached to it;

An aim is to establish a positive transference with extremely rare, if any, interpretation of transference;

A review of and interpretation of previous crises is done if they relate to the present one;

A strengthening of defenses and an emphasis on support;

The therapist is selectively directive and active in participation;

Environmental management and the use of social or family support is often great;

The treatment is eclectic within the bounds of its goals.

Open-ended (historically called "long-term") psychotherapy utilizes the methods of:

Focusing on past childhood experiences;

Maximizing the use of free association to reveal unconscious thoughts and processes;

Interpretation of transference feelings and behaviors;

Interpretation of early childhood determinants of present conflicts, behaviors, thoughts, and feelings;

An exploratory, interpretive approach with little support;

An emphasis on uncovering defenses;

Limited therapist involvement such that the therapist is fairly non-directive and less active;

Often psychoanalytic in its practice;

Environmental management is very rare.

Indicators

Indicators for the use of brief or very brief psychotherapy include: a state of emotional turmoil or distress that is related to a core conflict which is contributing to the distress. It may also be used for personal or professional growth and as a trial of therapy to see what the response is and how rapid it is.

The indicators for crisis intervention are the existence of the state of disequilibrium brought about by a disruptive crisis and/or loss resulting in acute emotional pain. It is contra-indicated for long-term, chronic, non-acute problems.

The indicators for open-ended or longer-term psychotherapy include more entrenched personality traits, greater severity of symptoms than is workable in brief psychotherapy, and those who will take longer to establish a therapeutic alliance than brief psychotherapy permits.

5.

Considerations Concerning Who Is Most Likely to Benefit from Brief Integrative Psychodynamic Treatment

If most psychotherapy is now brief, that is lasting for less than six months of weekly sessions, it appears there is a more useful question to ask than who can benefit from brief treatment (as opposed to more "open-ended" therapy). If the approach is a psychodynamically informed and integrative treatment, then it might be best to ask, "What are the characteristics of those who are most likely to benefit and in what period of time and with what particular elements to the treatment plan?" It is then, a matter of estimating probabilities and the variables most influencing those probabilities followed by designing a treatment plan with the specific elements to maximize the probabilities of the most improvement possible.

Original criteria would now be seen as archaic and ruled out the majority of outpatients such that David Malan's (1976) criteria left only 30-35% of outpatients eligible. He ruled out those with serious suicide attempts, drug addiction, "convinced homosexuality" (which was at that time in history seen as pathology), had had long-term hospitalization, more than one course of ECT, chronic alcoholism, incapacitating obsessional symptoms, incapacitating phobic symptoms, or gross destructive acts.

The criteria was broadened by Habib Davanloo (1978), a Malan protégé, and by Horowitz, Marmor, Krupnick, et al. (1984) to include more severe character pathology and more difficult patients. However, Peter Sifneos (1979) proposed a narrower criteria and added the requirements of high motivation for treatment, high trust in the therapist, low resistance, low defensiveness, and an "oedipal" type of problem; resulting in only 5-10% of outpatients being eligible. Thus, this criteria may select people who: 1) would get better on their own anyway, 2) would get better with any treatment, and/or 3) are compliant and report gains, improvement, satisfaction, and agree with the interpretations of the therapist.

As far back as 1984, Strupp and Binder found this criteria too limiting and they suggested the following criteria as does Levenson (2010) requiring the person to have:

1. Emotional discomfort (pain);

2. Basic trust (and hope);

3. Willingness to consider conflicts in interpersonal terms;

4. Willingness to examine feelings and is open to considering their importance;

5. Capacity for mature relationships;

    a. Sees others as separate individuals in their own right;

    b. Affect is not too isolated;

c. Mistrust not too great to rapidly form a working relationship;

6. Motivation for this treatment.

We might see if some of Strupp and Binder's identified traits are more evident in an extended evaluation of three or even four sessions.

Many note "good ego-strength". Although this is vague, the best meaning might be the degree of ability to tolerate and manage frustrations and obstacles while completing a longer-term task in life over a matter of months or years.

These earlier observations might be considered clinical lore not meeting today's standards of evidence. From an Evidence Based Medicine (EBM) perspective little of the above holds except the following (Wampold, 2010; Lambert, Hunt, & Vermeersch, 2004):

— Those with high *motivation* will be able to accomplish more in a shorter period of time. However, this motivation must be not just for symptom removal or a change that will simply decrease emotional pain. Rather, there must be a willingness to change how life is lived more broadly. Improvement is more likely for those motivated and ready to make fundamental changes in how they go about doing things in life and especially in their relationships;

- Those who are *able to form a more open, trusting and hopeful relationship with the therapist more rapidly* are most likely to have the greatest amount of gain in the least amount of time. This is a robust finding because the greatest single predictor of psychotherapy outcome is the quality of the therapeutic alliance. Of course, those who are avoidant or require a long period of time to develop adequate trust to engage in the work will be far less likely to be able to rapidly engage and thus will benefit less in a brief period of time;

- *Ego strength* as noted above including the degree of emotional, cognitive, and behavioral self-regulation in the completing of a long-term goal such as a job advancement training program or educational program with daily self-monitored tasks requiring the ability to tolerate both internal and external distress;

- *Psychological mindedness* or the ability to be aware of feelings and to be able to describe them;

- Additional *negative predictive factors* noted in recent meta-analytic reviews include: severe mood disorder, organic brain damage, psychosomatic symptoms, entrenched negativism and hostility, intense dependency needs, intense rigidity and/or perfectionism, the lack of external support from others, and the lack of a positive response to a trial of treatment (Wampold, 2010);

— Additionally, those with greater initial severity generally make fewer gains. *Severity* is meant to include the *duration* of the problem, the degree of *subjective distress*, the degree of *functional impairment,* as well as the *pervasiveness* or focality of the problem. All affect severity (Lambert, Hunt, & Vermeersch, 2004);

— Finally, those with problems regulating *eating, substance addictions, the after-effects of trauma, symptoms of psychosis, or strong personality traits that create problem situations*, may benefit some from brief treatment if the goal is targeted, circumscribed, and deemed to be achievable as a separate piece of work. For example, learning to recognize the inner states caused by a certain set of stressful event triggers and some self-soothing, emotion regulation techniques to practice and use as needed. Those with borderline or psychotic symptoms would generally receive only supportive or skill development elements with no push for recognition of patterns, etc. and especially no activity that might threaten the alliance such as analyzing the interactions with the therapist. With those whose problems are judged to be more severe, the key to the treatment may be in the selection of the micro-techniques.

In the assessment domain we would like to know what areas of life are affected and how as well as what areas are not affected or are less affected. Additionally, knowing when functioning and satisfaction in life have been better and when they have been worse as well as what circumstances and personal actions seem to influence these is beneficial for the treatment planning.

© J.E. Talley, Ph.D.

6.

Therapist Selection Criteria:
Who Can Do Brief Psychotherapy Better?

1. As in all systems of psychological treatment, the therapist who *believes in the effectiveness* of brief therapy will have the better outcome.

2. The therapist who is more comfortable being *active verbally and interactive* will be more likely to lead the person seeking help sufficiently with questions that bring the process to its outcome in less time. Some have seen this as a need to speak directively. Yet, more than coming across as the expert and authority, the general demeanor of confidence in one's abilities to guide the therapeutic tasks and the adequacy of the techniques in the context of the relationship to foster positive change should be evident.

3. *Therapist comfort with a more limited focus* (e.g., a symptom or two and a problematic interpersonal circumstance or "core conflictual relationship theme" as the goal and if there is more than one they should be clearly and closely related).

4. This also necessitates therapist *comfort with a more limited outcome by virtue of the more limited goals*. In this stance, however, there is also a decreased likelihood of a sense of failure since small gains are valued.

5. The therapist needs the ability to *come to a rapid assessment and focus*. Yet, everyone's diagnostic picture is always enriched and thus changed with the increased material that comes over time. Often more time with a person with the opportunity to observe their response to treatment is essential for an accurate assessment. Often, then, the assessment is less rapid and the person must be told that a more extended evaluation is necessary before treatment specifics can be discussed.

6. This treatment requires the therapist to have the skills to *translate symptoms into a determining problematic relationship theme that tends to recur*.

7. The therapist must be able to and preferably feel very comfortable establishing a *positive relationship* with the person seeking help while fostering a strong therapeutic alliance and an environment in which the person feels as safe and as comfortable as possible in order to collaboratively explore the focus.

8. Nevertheless, it is also preferable that the therapist feel *comfortable asking questions that are painful* or cause anxiety and at times the therapist may attempt to elicit unpleasant emotions in order to work with these emotions and facilitate mastery of them more fully. Thus, the therapist is better off when able to judiciously mix supportive and expressive (insight-oriented and emotionally activating) techniques.

9. *Flexibility* with the use of a variety of micro-techniques and interventions including gestalt, systems, strategic, behavioral, cognitive, emotion-focused, and interpersonal techniques is helpful.

10. Many of the therapist traits and actions that are optimal for open-ended psychotherapy are also optimal for brief psychotherapy such as the ability not only to empathize but also the *ability to convey empathy* to the other person that is recognized by them. This may be even more important in briefer work.

11. The ability to *take the lead in establishing common goals* that are generated by the person seeking help and also the ability to *take the lead in identifying the tasks and process by which progress toward those goals* or achievement of them will be made has been shown to be associated with a positive outcome as has the therapist inquiring how the person believes the work is going and the therapist giving feedback on progress made (Wampold, 2010). These two activities are therapist contribution components of the therapeutic alliance building as is the therapist's contribution to the sense of a bond of working together toward the common goals. This bond has been termed the "we bond" by Lester Luborsky, who has identified ways the therapist can strengthen that bond and was for decades the leader of the Pennsylvania Psychotherapy Research Project (Luborsky, 1984).

12. Better outcome has been shown to be influenced by the therapist *conveying hope for improvement, respect for the client, patient, or seeker and being motivated to attend to and help with their concerns* (Lambert & Anderson, 1996). These have all been found to be components of the therapeutic alliance as have the abilities to *convey warmth and to convey understanding*. The operative key word being "convey", although these factors have been difficult to tease out from each other (Horvath & Bedi, 2002). Flexible therapist responses and therapist responses that did *not engage in subtle hostility or a tendency to be controlling* were likewise indicators of positive outcome. (Lambert, Hunt, & Vermeersch, 2004; Najavits & Strupp, 1994).

13. Wampold (2011) notes from an evidence based perspective, therapists with the best outcomes:

    − Have a sophisticated set of interpersonal skills;

    − Build trust, understanding, and belief;

    − Have an alliance;

    − Have an acceptable and adaptive explanation of the condition presented;

    − Have a treatment plan that they allow to be flexible;

    − Are influential, persuasive, and convincing;

- Monitor progress;

- Offer hope and realistic optimism;

- Are reflective;

- Are aware of the person's characteristics in context;

- Rely on the best research evidence;

- Continually improve.

7.

The Underlying, Overarching Macro-Technique: General Treatment Interventions of the Therapist

1. Assist in defining the nature of the problem (including a careful and detailed history regarding interpersonal and intrapsychic circumstances affecting the presenting problem).

2. Establish a focus with the patient, client, or seeker as a "core conflictual relationship theme" (CCRT) (Luborsky & Crits-Christoph, 1990; Eells & Lombart, 2004) or a "cyclical maladaptive pattern" (CMP) (Levenson, 2010; Strupp & Binder, 1984; Binder, 2004); or a "configurational analysis" (CA) (Horowitz, Marmor, Krupnick, et al., 1984; Eells & Lombart, 2004). The focus is a core conflict, the problem under the problem, the most probable and greatest determinant/cause of the presenting problem.

3. Maintain the focus by bringing most new data, tangents, or related problems and other emotional, cognitive, or behavioral concerns back to the focus, weaving them into the fabric of the focus and thus enriching, deepening, and strengthening the focus.

4. Encourage/promote catharsis directly and indirectly (the stimulation and release of emotion).

5. Promote insight by linking the themes that occurred with parents and family to themes occurring with significant others and IF and

ONLY IF there is clear receptivity to it, with transferential manifestations of those themes with the therapist. (See section on transference about this.)

6. Promote the emotional experience associated with all insights and especially those concerning losses that may be or are associated with change and increased separation-individuation and/or differentiation.

7. Use the micro-techniques to assist in all of this.

8. Call attention very gently to defenses, avoidance, and reluctance or inhibition as appears acceptable to that person at that time.

9. Promote exploration and collaborative puzzling aloud with regard to possible causes and influences affecting the presenting problem.

10. Share hypotheses and "wonderings" (as opposed to making interpretations) or share tentative interpretations, explanations, and hunches.

11. Terminate in a positive fashion using the opportunity to link feelings about the separation back to the focus and core conflict.

12. Use the positive transference aspect of the relationship in the therapeutic alliance.

13. Five good focusing questions include:

1. What is the person trying to get from others in their interactions and what are they doing to try to obtain it?

2. How does the person expect others to respond?

3. How do others *actually* react to this? (What does the person *really get* as a response from others when they do what they think will result in getting what they want?)

4. How does the person then treat themselves internally following what the other person did in response to their initial action?

5. How does the person construe the relationship with me? How might their actions be a consequence of our previous interactions and how do I, the therapist, feel in response to the person?

14. Provide a "constructive experience in living" versus "a corrective emotional experience." (I know of no good evidence to suggest that personality structure can be completely changed or become "restructured." Traits and tendencies appear to be tamed by a matter of degree and usually by developing, activating, or freeing up counter-balancing parts of the personality as opposed to eradicating or totally suppressing character traits. The "constructive experience" is activating and additive more than "corrective" as I see it and this seems in accord with Milton Erickson's and Carl Jung's perspectives.)

15. Part of the developmental and transformational aspect of this treatment is to assist when possible in helping the other person move on to the next stage in life, even if only in part, along a continuum. Thus, there might be some aim to help the adolescent who wishes to be perfect to consolidate their identity as less than perfect, although they may move into young adulthood looking for perfection in intimacy (since giving up on the wish for perfection in all ways may be rejected). Likewise with increasing age the quest for perfection may move forward into the tasks of creativity, generativity, and wisdom.

16. Establish an agreement about treatment length as well as the roles and responsibilities of each party. While it is doubtful that therapists can fully make up for parental deprivations no matter how long the therapy lasts, it is even more unlikely to occur in brief treatment. Rather, it seems likely that all therapists, like all parents, will eventually disappoint in some way. The question is — can the therapist empathize with negative feelings the other person is having about them? This was in all likelihood not done by the parents but it can be done well in brief psychotherapy. This can promote greater tolerance of frustration as the therapist is seen accepting and empathizing with these negative feelings. Such therapist empathy will deepen the therapeutic alliance, promote greater self-acceptance, and make it more likely that the frustrations and disappointments the person feels in response to others will be better tolerated.

17. Offer and foster hope by indirect or direct encouragement (e.g., "I'm optimistic that together, we can work to make some progress on this.")

8.

Specific Micro-Techniques Useable in Brief Psychotherapy

(Electicism and integrationism regarding technique does not imply the same regarding theory.)

1. Relaxation exercises;

2. Biofeedback;

3. Meditation;

4. Cognitive-Behavioral Therapy (CBT) such as the work of Aaron Beck, the analysis of thought patterns, clarifying underlying guiding assumptions and beliefs about the self, the world and others;

5. Associations to dream figures;

6. Dialoging with dream figures;

7. Gestalt techniques like "talking to the empty chair" (dialogues with another or with part of the self);

8. Using metaphors, tales, and stories;

9. The affect bridge technique tying current feelings associated with problematic emotional states and the core conflictual relationship theme (CCRT);

10. Eliciting of the earliest memories (this and the affect bridge may help determine a focus and/or CCRT);

11. Shifting perspective via trance, hypnotic environment, or Ericksonian communication and methods;

12. Using guided imagery;

13. Using spontaneous imagery and active imagination such as the inner guide technique;

14. Paradoxes (true ones may be the best);

15. Systematic desensitization and exposure techniques;

16. Modeling;

17. Promoting increased self-esteem when needed and appropriate by truthful observations about accomplishments and attributes (can be tricky);

18. Specific self-disclosure (being mindful that the meaning can be taken differently);

19. Psycho-educational comments;

20. Environmental change/considerations (e.g., vocational counseling and/or change or couple/family relations counseling);

21. Adjunct group therapy;

22. Adjunct pharmacological treatment;

23. Hypnotic methods including self-hypnosis and any behavioral or other technique that does not undermine the therapist's basic stance of acceptance, support, and collaborative constructor of meanings and possibilities (e.g., using terms like "irrational beliefs" may come across too critically);

24. A handshake at the end of each hour is often felt to be very supportive;

25. Assertiveness training;

26. Identifying and labeling "parts" of the self, especially those parts that might be in conflict with each other;

27. Bibliotherapy;

28. Identifying and labeling images of person-part and feeling associations with each with regard to others;

29. Most any other therapy micro-technique including:
    a. Emotion Focused Therapy (EFT) techniques;
    b. Interpersonal Psychotherapy (IPT) techniques;
    c. Dialectical Behavioral Therapy (DBT) techniques;
    d. Acceptance and Commitment Therapy (ACT) techniques.

© J.E. Talley, Ph.D.

9.

Assessment and Evaluation: The Initial Sessions

Treatment begins the moment the therapist meets the other person, even if the therapist construes it as an assessment or evaluation. This is true because the quality of the therapeutic alliance is the single greatest predictor of therapy outcome (Horvath & Bedi, 2002) and this working relationship begins the moment the two parties meet.

The primary aim of the therapist then is to promote rapport and engage the other person while secondarily gaining the most relevant information. No matter how wonderful the evaluation is, if the person doesn't return, treatment is over. Thus, the main aim of the first session must be to promote the likelihood of a second session.

After introductions, the therapist might guide the opening by asking something like, "What brings you in today?" or "How might I be of use to you, etc.?" in a way that invites the one seeking assistance to tell the story of what has brought them to the appointment. All questions by the therapist that follow are best when it is not too difficult to imagine that the answer to the question will aide in providing a greater understanding of an aspect of the presenting concern. This keeps all inquiry seemingly related to the presenting concern, which helps to strengthen the alliance.

Our observations of the person as they respond in addition to the content of the response will help us conclude the probabilities of a more successful outcome to psychotherapy in a brief period of time and the necessary components of this particular brief psychotherapy to maximize the probability of a successful outcome.

- Assign priority to the person's functioning in the interview and current relationships outside treatment, and

- Then, but to a lesser extent, to thematically similar problems in earlier relationships on back to those in the family of origin.

The goal of the evaluation is not simply a formal diagnosis, although that may also be done, but rather a formulation concerning how the person seems to think or feel and then act in ways that leave others responding in such a manner that problematic interpersonal scenarios or themes are repeated. These repetitions, in turn, result in other symptoms, problems, or concerns that in some way leave the person's efforts, aims, or intentions seemingly thwarted, defeated, or self-defeated.

Kinds of data obtained include:

1. A few questions covering the nature of current and prior problems, complaints, and symptoms including the details and history of these and of similar problems had by family members broadened to include grandparents, aunts, uncles and first cousins especially if treated professionally;

2. A mental status examination that may be formal or informal depending on the setting and how innocuously it can be completed;

3. A history of past significant relationships in some detail (e.g., romances, roommates, and family);

4. Information about current relationships including both positive and negative associated feelings and their causes;

5. Observations about transactions in the therapeutic relationship.

   - Avoid an approach or stance that seems too fact-finding with a detective-like manner, or as one who's in the know, etc.

   - Create an atmosphere of mutual puzzling, curiosity, and collaboration.

Sample Questions for Initial Sessions

1. What brings you in this morning? Where would you like to begin?

2. What *specifically* has happened that caused you to come in *now* at this time?

3. Is this the first time you've ever had this problem or a similar problem?

4. How long has it been going on?

ASSESSMENT AND EVALUATION: THE INITIAL SESSIONS

5. What circumstances might be influencing the problem now? At earlier times?

6. How did you manage it before?

7. Does it seem that this difficulty in any way has anything to do with your relationships with other people? (The relationship themes may need to be puzzled about with information given in response to other questions.)

8. Tell me a bit about where you work (or go to school) and what's that like for you?

9. Do you have some friends or acquaintances there?

10. How would you describe those people?

11. How would you describe your relationships with them?

12. What do you do for fun (or with your spare time)?

13. Who are the people you're closest to?

14. Can you describe in more detail your relationship with (e.g., Bill, Sally, and Sue)?

15. Did you have some other friends? How did things go with them?

16. How would you describe your family?

17. What was it like growing up in your family of origin?

18. Tell me a bit about your (e.g., mother, father, sister, brother).

19. What significant losses have you experienced in your life? Major disappointments?

20. What other important life disruptions have you experienced?

21. Describe what you experience in your more intimate relationships, one at a time.

22. How does sexuality enter into your relationships with others with (e.g., Jack, Jill, and Ronald)?

23. What haven't I asked about yet that might be important for me to understand or know about you?

Obvious follow-up questions to any others:

        a. Can you say some more about that?

        b. What's that like for you?

        c. What do you make of that?

        d. What's your sense of how that came about?

Each evaluation would not include many of these questions and, of course, the response to one question generates another very often not on this list.

The most significant questions are probably those concerning the onset of the problem and the particular external and internal corresponding (or preceding) events.

10.

The Therapeutic Alliance

Summarizing the empirically supported aspects of the alliance, Wampold and Budge (2012) note that the strength of the alliance is a function of the therapist being perceived as trustworthy, understanding, and possessing expertise.

To enhance the alliance Wampold (2010) offers the five points below:

1. Help the person define their goals for the work together;

2. Come to an agreement with the person as to how those goals will be worked toward or the tasks that will be engaged in. These two points above and the "we bond" have been shown to be the basic ingredients in the alliance determining therapy outcome and therefore are most essential for the therapist to attend to;

3. Therapists with better outcomes formed better alliances and therapist contributions to the alliance were predictive of outcome whereas patient, client, or seeker contributions and patient, client, or seeker and therapist interaction contributions were not;

4. Attending to progress, monitoring it and expressing it to the person was a contributing factor to the alliance and predictive of more positive outcome;

5. The therapist communicating hope (realistic optimism) that the person will make progress and expressing this while the therapist modulated their own emotions was also predictive of positive outcome as was the therapist's ability to perceive the patient, client, or seeker's emotional state and to create a collaborative relationship.

The below clinical lore or wisdom has been summarized by Bauer and Kobos (1993):

1. The alliance helps to maintain motivation for therapy. It mitigates and contains frustrations arising in therapy;

2. For brief therapy, it is not optimal that long work aimed at building the alliance need to be a focus or major goal itself and therefore, those requiring much time aimed at establishing an adequate alliance probably will require a more open-ended therapy;

3. Having no alliance leads to a therapeutic impasse and stalemate;

4. The alliance needs to be a mutually respectful and trusting container to look at interactions, including those with the therapist without rejection by the therapist when the patient, client, or seeker is angry with the therapist;

5. So the person must become attached to therapist and experience a sense of bond that "*we*" are working on the task together;

6. They paraphrase Freud's original thoughts on the alliance as follows: The therapist must: (1) exhibit a serious interest in the person's concerns, (2) clear away "resistance", avoidance, reluctance (obstacles) as they develop, (3) be nonjudgmental and as objective as possible, and (4) help the person identify with the therapist as a fellow collaborator in therapy;

7. The therapist needs to be compassionate and sensitive to the person's sense of dignity and integrity as a human being such that rules or regulations are not imposed without explanation;

8. While stimulating curiosity about symptoms and self, the therapist is stable and consistent without being rigid or wooden.

Additionally, the therapist should:

1. Attend to the alliance from the outset by conveying empathy and discussing fears, misgivings, and misconceptions about therapy;

2. Use naturally occurring positive transference feelings;

3. Convey unqualified acceptance and interest in the person (even during any assessment phase if one exists). Being "objective" or "neutral" or very nondirective may be interpreted easily as a lack of acceptance. Convey an open and warm attitude;

4. Actively encourage verbalization;

    - Interrupt prolonged periods of silence with exploration;

- If silence continues, consider its avoidant function;

5. Convey your understanding of the person as soon as possible even if tentative and wonder about it together to titrate and moderate anxiety;

6. Wonder aloud (rather than "interpret") about the possibility of negative relationship phenomena if there is apparent hostility, fear, or a sense of threat that the therapist may or may try to control them. Additionally, discuss concerns about and dissatisfactions with the therapist early and in a way that defuses by implying such feelings are common. This is an extraordinarily delicate task and care needs to be taken that the person not feel blamed or as if feelings are being pinned on them. It is best to leave this undone if the means does not seem available and if it may put the alliance at risk;

    - Ideally, bringing out negative reactions into the open for discussion will prevent leaving them unattended, which can lead to dropping out of therapy. But, "easy does it" is best with these matters.

7. Convey a sense of hopeful optimism (not superficially, but realistically) directly and/or indirectly;

8. Discuss the roles of both parties in therapy and the therapy process, noting the person's more active role and therapy as collaborative. Help the person see that one task is to discover

how conflicted thoughts and feelings lead to problems in living. There may be information given about coping mechanisms (defenses), anxiety, and outside of awareness feelings as well as using here and now interchanges with the therapist. Again, there is risk here of negative outcome when interpreting transference that is now documented (see the notes on transference);

9. Show a spirit of collaboration in manner too. For insights to be most valuable, they need to be grounded (ideally) in immediate experience with the therapist too;

10. I would note again that what has been termed therapist "neutrality" understandably feels like neglect or indifference. Arguably, they are correct. Thus, it is unworkable to expect another to accept that their response to this is a "negative transference". Neutrality probably works against building an alliance;

11. Transference cannot be distinctly separated from the alliance or from the "real" relationship, so be attuned to possible transferential feelings especially if they might be disruptive or alliance threatening;

12. Because of the preceding point, the therapeutic alliance fluctuates throughout therapy, even at times moment-to-moment as a function of the transference component, so transference is a help but also at times, hinders. Attend carefully to such pulls without engaging in them as struggles.

See also Bennett and Parry (2004); Horvath and Bedi (2002); Lambert and Barley (2002); Crits-Christoph and Gibbons (2002) and Norcross (2002).

11.

Establishing the Focus

The focus of brief integrative psychodynamic psychotherapy is a theme summarizing the basic "cyclical maladaptive pattern" (CMP) (Levenson, 2010; Binder, 2004); "core conflictual relationship theme" (CCRT) of Lester Luborsky and Paul Crits-Christoph (1990) also described by Eells and Lombart (2004); or "configurational analysis"(CA) also summarized by Eells and Lombart (2004) that tends to be repeated with significant others throughout life and is ultimately attempted in some version with the therapist.

If the presenting complaint is a feeling or a troublesome physical ailment, then a detailed behavioral analysis of its history and its context is vital in order to see if the somatic complaint or the dysphoria has its origin in or is maintained by problems with regard to relating with others.

Questions focused on what was occurring at the time of and just before the onset of the problem or symptom across several recent occurrences are essential. Questions concerning what thoughts were going on or might have been operative (in some form, perhaps outside of awareness) for such feelings to occur, are also useful.

Ascertaining what is or might be in some odd way "good" about having the problem and what might be or would be different without the problem including how that change might be not so good, may also elucidate the problem's interpersonal underpinnings. Asking,

"What would it really be like if your wish came true – what might be bad about it coming true?" is often informative as is an exploration of what this problem helps the person avoid, especially in relation to others?

If a CCRT cannot be identified as a focus, then some other form of treatment (e.g., behavioral, hypnotic, biofeedback, pharmacological) is indicated to focus primarily on symptom relief.

The CCRT puts together what the presenting person wishes for with others and is afraid of in relation to others with regard to that wish. The conflict between the wish and the fear is explored as to how it may relate to, generate, or maintain the problem. For example, the person may for various reasons, understandable given the events of the person's life, have a wish to exert a degree of control or influence over what they do with others, but they also may fear that if they succeed in doing this, then they would not be liked. The person may have a corresponding feeling, for example, that they must be liked by the other(s) involved. Thus, the first steps would be, "I'd like to exert some influence over where X and I go, but I'm afraid that if I do, X won't like me." This thought shows a conflict between a wish and a fear associated with acting to fulfill the wish.

Continuing this formulation would move to a statement concerning how the person will then feel towards themselves and toward the other person, "then I'll feel foolish and irritated with X." Next, some probably unacknowledged decision is made concerning how to manage this dilemma that tries to have it all, usually by hedging bets and not opting definitively for either side of the dilemma which would require a tough decision. The person then at some level of the mind tries to have it all by saying something like, "So I'll just try to keep my feelings to myself. It's not worth causing any trouble about."

This attempt at suppression is eventually not effective as the tension between the wish and the fear intensifies with the result that the tension then "leaks" out in the form of the "symptom" or the problematic behavior, feeling, or thought (see Triangle 1). These themes manifest themselves with others (see Triangle 2).

Mardi Horowitz's "configurational analysis" (Eells & Lombart, 2004) enriches this with: (1) the aim (a wish or want), "I want X from (another person) but, (2) I have Y, (these fears, inhibitions, impediments, personal deficiencies or problems, and (3) if I get what I want then I'll have A (an internal positive response) and/or B (an external positive response), but if I get what I want then I may also have C (an internal negative response) and D (an external negative response), so I am ambivalent and in inner conflict and therefore will try to cover all the bases/all options using these (self-defeating) coping strategies and the results will be:

- recurrent states of mind 1, 2 and 3 (including unmodulated, well modulated, and overly modulated states)
- recurrent feelings A, B, C, and D (above)

- recurrent interpersonal scenarios and back-up scenarios X, Y, and Z."

For example, I want (wish for) some control over what happens at work, but I'm not very persuasive and if I get what I want I might feel good and effective and be respected more, but I'll get burned out since I'd get more responsibility and work to do, so I'll not speak up yet and try to be liked and get a raise some other way (dressing better) which leads, for example, to feeling apathetic at meetings.

The essence of all of this (portrayed in triangle 1) is that a thought about acting to fulfill a wish gives rise to a fear which then creates a state of inner conflict characterized by feeling ambivalent and being stuck concerning action. The conflict results in a problematic way of trying to get what one wants while simultaneously trying to avoid a felt danger.

(Some believe that if we wish for something, a part of us also fears it, and if we fear something, a part of us also wishes for it.)

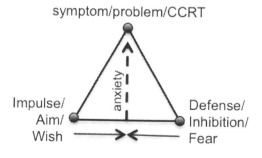

Triangle 1

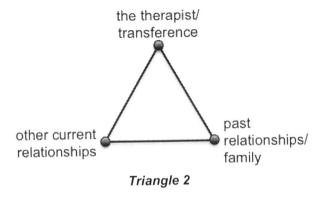

Triangle 2

We need to come to understand how this symptom, problem, or CCRT is a creating pain or discomfort and also how it enables the person to avoid or believe that they will avoid something they fear would be even worse. As a compromise of sorts, the problem permits one to hedge their bets and feel as if the gains might be had while also avoiding the risks. Yet, the result is that although what was feared may be avoided, in doing so, that which was wanted was also missed. Whatever was wanted might have been had if a full, un-ambivalent effort to obtain it had been made and there are usually other unintended negative consequences to the compromise action.

- The symptom or problem is an attempt of sorts to solve another problem but the person stays stuck at an impasse or is "accelerating with the brakes on".

- In order to change the situation, the payoff or benefit (transacted under the inner table and outside of full acknowledgement) usually needs to become more apparent and the responsibility accepted for both the good and the not so desirable aspects of the outcome resulting from whatever choice is made, even if made by passivity and default.

- *If the wish might be seen as more of an aspiration than an expectation and if the fears can be contained or decreased with various exercises and practices, then the intensity of the conflict and subsequently the severity of the symptom might be decreased.* Then for further gain, we come up against the roots and toughest part. The person has to either:

1. Defend against anxiety or frustration in a new way other than the present problem, such as channeling tension from the conflict into creative love, play, work, or another problem;
2. Realize and accept that the wishes are unlikely to be fulfilled and impossible to completely satisfy (or maybe at all);
3. Decrease or let go of the fears and inhibitions about acting to achieve the wishes, perhaps by decreasing the belief in the likelihood of the fears coming true or how terrible it would be if the fears came true;
4. Utilize some combination or balance of 1, 2 and 3;
5. For those ready, transform the wishes to a different, higher order problem (e.g., seek the ideal and perfection via creative expression) instead of with the "perfect" romance so that some bit or essential element of the wish is retained while its means or form is altered or transformed.

This is very difficult since wishes, fears, and defenses are intertwined with the whole personality and are developed in the context of close relationships with great attachment (e.g., family). Thus, there may be feelings of threat and/or loss with the change or modification of them.

- A separation/individuation or differentiation from the family of origin and from part of the self is usually involved intrapsychically to some degree.
- There may be some or quite a bit of biological influence at play.

But with the recognition of the value or "payoff" of the problem, one may feel more accepting of it and negative feelings about the self are reduced when the problem is seen as "understandable" and "reasonable" given the context, circumstances, and alternatives. Part of maintaining the payoff is that the person can retain the belief that a better option will come about later that permits actualizing the wishes at less or no risk. This permits acting *as if* things are true that by observation, experience, and experimentation do not appear to be true.

As summarized by Eells and Lombart (2004), studies (e.g.,Crits-Christoph, Cooper, & Luborsky, 1988) have supported the establishment and maintenance of a focus as a predictor of positive outcome if that focus is accurate concerning the person's main wishes and hoped for responses from others. Additional studies (Piper, Joyce, McCallum, & Azim, 1993; Høgland & Piper, 1995;

Joyce & Piper, 1996) support the use of a focus as a predictor of positive outcome if transference interpretations are at a low frequency.

For a review of the efficacy of psychodynamic psychotherapy see Shedler (2010).

Examples of a Focus with a Core Conflictual Relationship Theme (CCRT)

1. "I wish to be close to others, but I fear that if I am, they'll have expectations of me and then if I do as they wish, I'll loose autonomy as well as resent them (the feeling of the self towards the other) and not respect myself (the feeling of the self toward the self) for just going along. On the other hand, if I do what would please me more, then I'll be seen as selfish, not be liked and be treated poorly by them in return. So in order to avoid these problems (and avoid the anxiety of this conscious choice) as well as the other problems that would follow, I'll just avoid people and not have to deal with their expectations of me and not be placed in what feels like a 'no win' situation." The avoidant style resulting from the above theme was a defense to cope with the conflicting wish and fear. However, when it didn't work and someone intruded or was present in a way that was difficult to avoid and the person perceived an expectation by others, they would develop an incapacitating headache (presenting symptom) or one that greatly diminished their capacities and would then

feel trapped and resentful but unable to do anything about it for fear of the consequences. This was the conflict theme that appeared in varying forms with parents, romantic relationships, co-workers, supervisors, and the therapist.

2. "I wish for intimacy with a commitment, but I fear that if I get a romantic partner, I might lose them. They could leave me for another, stay and withdraw emotionally, or perhaps die young, so I'll only become attached to someone if I already sense (outside of conscious awareness) that I can never fully have them because they have another, one or both of us will be leaving soon, or I intuit that it can never really work out." These issues seem to matter only as commitment becomes a real possibility. Then the fact that the potential partner may have a serious problem, is highly ambivalent about commitment themselves, or is different in some way such as political party, ethnicity, or religion that the person would never really be fully comfortable with, may come to feel like a more significant factor and grounds to end the relationship.

3. "I wish for intimacy with commitment, but I fear that if I get a romantic partner, I might lose them, so as a new relationship gets more serious, I'll feel less anxious if I have another relationship as a back-up in case I lose this one (which, of course, is likely to fracture the first relationship)."

4. "I wish for a loving, intimate relationship but I fear the other person will become too dependent on me and be too needy of me and I fear (usually outside of awareness) that will mean my own dependency wishes (unrecognized) will never get met. I also fear getting swallowed up in the relationship and not being able to do other things I want to do. So, I'll find someone very self-sufficient who won't need me too much." After some time of this romantic partner, if found, our person presents again but with complaints of a lack of closeness in the relationship in part due to the partner's discomfort showing vulnerability. Of course, this was just what the person had been looking for. Alternatively, our person might present with complaints that their partner is too controlling and then the person might fear that they will lose their own identity, autonomy, and separateness. They might think, "I'll find a partner who is very accepting, undemanding and wants to please me." This time the person presents with complaints that the partner can't be counted on to take care of things on their own, is too passive, and too dependent, or not successful on their own. The defense for both of these may be to look for the opposite or the ever-elusive more perfect balance.

© J.E. Talley, Ph.D.

12.

Some Standard Core Conflictual Relationship Theme (CCRT) Categories

Some standard core conflictual relationship theme categories representing wishes and/or fears noted by Luborsky and Crits-Christoph (2003, p. 46) and modified are as follows:

"to be understood (… comprehended, … empathized with, … seen accurately);

to be accepted (… approved of, to not be judged, to be affirmed);

to be respected (… valued, … treated fairly, … be important to others);

to accept others (to be receptive to others);

to respect others (to value others);

to have trust (others to be honest, … genuine);

to be liked (others to be interested in me);

to be opened up to (… responded to, … talked to);

to be open (… express myself, … communicate);

to be distant from others (to not express myself/my feelings, to be left alone);

to be close to others (to be included, not to be left alone, to be friends);

to help others (to nurture others, to give to others);

to be helped (… nurtured, … given support, … given something valuable, to be protected);

to not be hurt (… avoid pain, avoid aggravation, and rejection, to protect/defend myself);

SOME STANDARD CORE CONFLICTUAL RELATIONSHIP THEME (CCRT) CATEGORIES

to be hurt (... punished, ... treated badly, ... injured);

to hurt others (... get revenge, ... reject others, ... express anger at others);

to avoid conflict (to compromise, not to anger others, ... get along, ... be flexible);

to oppose others (to resist domination, ... compete against others);

to have control over others (to dominate, ... have power, ... have things my own way);

to be controlled by others (to be submissive, ... dependent, ... passive, ... given direction);

to have self-control (to be consistent, ... rational);

to achieve (... be competent, ... win);

to be independent (... self-sufficient, ... self-reliant, ... autonomous);

to feel good about myself (... be self-confident, ...accept myself, ... have a sense of well-being);

to better myself (... improve, to get well);

to be good (... do the right thing, ...be perfect, ... be correct);

to be like other (... identify with other, ... be similar to other, ... model after other);

to be my own person (not to conform, to be unique)."

© J.E. Talley, Ph.D.

13.

Some Thoughts on Transference, Immediacy, and "Here and Now" Work in the Relationship

1. In brief dynamic treatment, it has been agreed generally that transferential material or interpersonal style behavior should be attended to (discussed, explored, wondered about aloud together) very soon, if not immediately, assuming the behavior appears to be related to the self-defeating pattern identified as the focus. An ample amount of research (Ogrodniczuk & Piper, 2004; Bennett & Parry, 2004; Binder, 2004; Ogrodniczuk, Piper, Joyce & McCallum, 1999) now calls the interpreting of transference in psychotherapy into question.

   Piper, Azim, Joyce, and McCallum (1991) found that a greater proportion of transference interpretations were related to a weaker therapeutic alliance and a less successful outcome in patients with high-quality object relations (QOR). Disturbingly, the findings, although not statistically significant for low-QOR patients, were, nevertheless, similar. To muddle these conclusions still further, Winston, McCullough, & Laikin, (1993) found that patients with more mature object relations did respond positively to active work on the transference while patients with less mature object relations responded to transference interpretations with hurt, anger, and withdrawal.

Høgland, Sorlie, Heyerdahl, Sorbye, and Amlo (1993) found that persistent analysis of the transference had a negative effect on long-term dynamic change at a four-year follow-up even for patients deemed highly suitable to receive transference interpretations. They conclude that transference interpretations should be used sparingly, with great care, and only with the particular needs of the individual patient as the determinant. Høgland (1993) also found that high QOR patients who had received frequent use of transference interpretations had a less favorable outcome.

Connolly, Crits-Christoph, Shappell, Barber, Luborsky, and Shaffer (1999) found that high levels of transference interpretations may be causally related to poor treatment outcome for some patients. This held true even though the percentage of transference interpretations was only one fourth of one percent of all therapist comments. The potential for a strong negative reaction by the person and feeling blamed is high as is the corresponding risk of drop-out from treatment. Binder (2004) has recommended that the therapist stay in a coaching and role-playing mode while analyzing the patients themes with others outside of the therapeutic relationship given these risks.

2. If transferential work is to be attempted, it might be facilitated by introducing the notion that you would like "permission" (to avoid control issues being activated) to inquire about and discuss things that go on between you and the patient/client, "Since

things that happen outside the office with other people often occur in some form in the office with me, so it'll help our work together if we can be free and open to exploring such things".

Particularly focusing on the person's thoughts and feelings about the therapeutic relationship rather than their behavior with the therapist would seem to help prevent feelings of blame.

3. Then, when something occurs indicating a possible thought or feeling, stopping traffic at the end of the phrase, sentence or idea and approaching it by saying for example, "When you said X just now, how were you feeling right then?" (Keeping it in the immediate past initially should be less threatening), and later perhaps... "How are you feeling right now?" and perhaps finally, if all has gone well," When you said X, I noticed that you ...", "What feelings were going on inside of you then?" followed with, for example, "What do those feelings remind you of?" or "When have you felt like that before?" If nothing emerges, then wondering by the therapist may be useful, for example, "Is it possible those feelings may be in any way related to the themes we've been looking at?" This leaves the person with a greater sense of control than the therapist sharing their sense of it first or then saying, "Would it be fair to say you're feeling a little X or Y or Z?" or "I imagine you might feel somewhat____ , " but done quite tentatively and not using terms reflecting primitive or strong emotions.

4. To extract a fantasy from a patient's question about the therapist, the therapist can say, "I'll be glad to respond to that question if it seems to be in your best interest to do so (if you are), but first, it'll help our work if we can understand what it would mean to you or how you would feel if I was _____ and how you'd feel if I wasn't. Can you tell me what you might make of it if I was _____?" This can also be done about a trait such as the patient's seeing the therapist as cold or uncaring. Also, "stupid" questions by the therapist can clarify. "Let me ask you a stupid question?" and "What do you make of it that I may smile too much?"

5. A continuous pursuit as Davanloo (1978) recommends even if done gently, caringly, with compassionate sensitivity, and without being at all argumentative or contentious seems risky depending on the findings from the above explorations.

6. A rupture in the alliance becomes likely if the therapist attempts to prove the patient's perception isn't accurate or to debate or contend about a perceived reality even subtly. Instead of, "If I seem _____ to you" the therapist might even try, "If I were (am) _____, what would that mean to you?"

7. Of course, if the therapist has needs to be seen in a certain way(s), this makes dealing with the transferential aspects more difficult perhaps by therapist collusion not to explore potentially negative material in the transference or in the "real relationship",

if that can be separated out. It seems suspect if the therapist feels that the affection, idealization, and caring toward the therapist is all in the real relationship and that the hostility, devaluing, and bad feeling toward the therapist are all taken as transferential. It has seemed to me that both the positive and the negative emotions the patient has toward the therapist will be felt by the therapist at about the same magnitude even if this isn't conscious in the mind of the therapist. What is counter-transference versus a counter-response that ninety-five percent of people would feel in reaction to what was said or done?

8. Don't avoid negative material or hints of it. If nothing is forthcoming, elicit it to get it on the table by way of active, kind, and gentle wondering aloud about the possibilities of what the person might be thinking or feeling inside and how all thoughts and feelings that might seem unusual in some contexts are quite "understandable" in light of the circumstances the person is in.

9. Help the person sit with the feelings around this and the feelings about the feelings (for example, feelings of guilt or fear about feeling anger) and help the person replay it with you in a less self-defeating, more successful, empowering, and healing way. For example, taking pride in their being assertive with you on some occasion if getting over avoidance was a goal. Help the person get there with some micro-techniques too. This may involve some behavioral and/or gestalt micro-techniques.

10. If transference material appears to have resulted in a rupture of the alliance or a therapeutic impasse emerges then Safran and Muran (2000) recommend that the therapist approach the experience with genuine curiosity, tentativeness, and an exploratory attitude that engages the person to collaborate in coming up with an understanding of the impasse or prior misunderstanding without making any parallels to outside relationships and that the therapist be aware that initial attempts to resolve an impasse will often initiate additional ruptures.

11. Wampold and Budge (2012) find the real relationship is one of three main pathways "through which the positive outcomes of psychotherapy are obtained".

12. What is transferential? How about as a guideline —when an affect seems greater than would be seen as warranted in a given situation by more than 95% or 90% (or whatever you like) of 100 people of same demographics as the reacting person, then it may be "transferential" or influenced by history. Redundancy and repetition in addition to intensity are keys indicating that the material is significant and may be likely to be transferential.

© J.E. Talley, Ph.D.

14.

Affect Bridge Technique

The affect bridge technique was first published by Watkins (1971) as a hypnoanalytic therapy technique, but can be very potent in bringing forth more powerful affect associated with the problem even without the use of hypnosis.

The amplified emotion then helps to show the client, patient, or seeker that the problem or "symptom" has an important history and that significant, related matters may be or have been outside of their awareness.

It also demonstrates experientially that the therapist has some understandings and techniques that can be very effective and thus, the belief that therapy may really be helpful is strengthened.

This in turn tends to heighten motivation and hopefulness; thus, building a spiral upward of positive expectations, trust in the therapist, etc.

This procedure may also ratify or validate the accuracy or meaningfulness of the chosen focus as we tend to believe that our feelings do not lie to us. This display of the associated feelings tends to erode denial that the problem is significant and/or the belief that the problem is not influenced by prior life experiences.

The tool might be used as the person is telling of the problem as they see it. When they reach an emotional climax and emote in some way the therapist nods with affirmation of interest and says, "Mmm-hmm, yes, now could you just, for a moment focus on that feeling and let it build a bit and describe it to me in some more detail." The affect bridge may be used when no emotion is present, but probably with less effect.

The therapist continues, "It may help if you close your eyes. See if you can describe it so vividly that it would be as if you could take me there with you as you picture the scene in your mind's eye."

"Perhaps you experience this feeling in some way as a sensation in certain parts of your body. Tell me about that." This is to activate "somatic memory" which is used in childhood particularly. The use of "perhaps" and "can" is to offer an implied suggestion that is soft with the intention of circumventing inner obstacles.

When the person has reached what the therapist senses to be a peak in the description, the therapist continues, "Good, thank you (a positive reinforcement). Now as you hold that very feeling, listening to the sound of my voice, let a part of your mind's eye detach itself and go backward in time... backward in time... as if your life were on a long video, until you find another memory, of a time, an experience, whatever comes to mind, in which you had the same or *similar* feelings or feelings that remind you of those feelings, a memory that carries this same or a similar feeling, that has the same or similar physical sensations or sensations that remind you of those sensations in some way. Just take whatever comes up. Nod when you have found it so that I'll know...but take your time." When the person nods, the therapist says, "Good. Thank you." reinforcing it.

"Now see if you can recall another such memory perhaps even earlier in time ... in which you had the same or similar sensations and feelings or feelings that remind you of these feelings. Just nod when you have it so that I'll know... but take your time." (pause for nod and then) "Good and how about another etc.?" repeating the last paragraph until about three to five memories of experiences have been gathered if possible. Then the therapist lets the person tell each memory in some detail, attempting to puzzle out a repetitive pattern or theme common to most or all of them and to see how those that are not repetitive of a theme may be related in some way.

Of particular interest is the identification of a core conflictual relationship theme (CCRT) along the lines described by Luborsky and Crits-Christoph (1990), or cyclical maladaptive pattern (CMP) described by Levenson (2010), Binder (2004), and originally by Strupp and Binder (1984). Can similar desires, wishes, aims, and intentions along with conflicting fears, inhibitions, and avoidances, as well as their corresponding symptoms, compromises, and conflicts with associated emotions be found among the elicited memories?

The affect bridge highlights an emotional echo and has an effect, in part, similar to the effect on a child who yells into a vast canyon and some moments later for the first time hears their own voice return as an echo, unmistakably their own voice, but seemingly coming from nowhere as if it has been suspended in time. There is an element of surprise and intrigue with the first experience of an echo making one want to try it again and play with it.

The affect bridge also operates like a rubber band stretched between a person's two hands as the opposing poles. The inquirer comes to therapy with a pain in one hand (which is in the relative present) that hurts more because it has been amplified by the 'pop' received when the other hand (in the relative past) let go of the rubber band as the event in the present jarred the stretched rubber band loose from the anchor in the past. Then the emotional force from the past snapped forward into the present. The affect bridge reverses the process (present to past) in a controlled, supportive setting that thus makes the rubber band (connecting two episodes with a similar theme) apparent as a link between the past and the present and across experiences.

The affect bridge is also exemplified by a very ripe peach falling to the floor and bruising. If a pointed sharp object then pokes all over the peach and we were to observe where the pointed object most easily penetrates the peach, we would find that the new sharp, pointed poke is most likely to penetrate the peach where it has been bruised earlier. The peach is more easily "hurt" or damaged when the new cut occurs on top of an old wound. Today's emotional wound hurts more when it occurs in the same place as an older bruise.

The person may be asked to simply share the earliest memory of feeling the problem feeling and then the four or five next earliest memories of feeling that way or similarly. Further, the person's earliest five to seven memories of anything may reveal a significant theme or conflict and associated coping patterns. The same may be true of their earliest memories of mother, father, etc. Key questions in exploring earliest memories and about anything to understand the person better in general include:

- What led up to this situation?

- How did you feel about (a significant person) in the memory?

- How did you sense she (or he) was feeling toward or about you?

- What happened (or might have happened if it cannot be recalled) next as an outcome or result of the situation?

- What might you as a child of that age have decided then in the back of your mind or out of your awareness about yourself, others, and the world?

- How would you describe your way of coping in the memory?

- What seems to have been the result of using that means of coping?

© J.E. Talley, Ph.D.

15.

Metaphors of the Problem

The use of a metaphor of the presenting problem or the person's situation can often help in getting a different type of understanding of the concern.

1. The little boy and the goose (below) may be used with any approach/avoidance problem such as intimacy.

    "I don't know if you have ever seen the picture, but in an introduction to psychology book there's a picture of a little boy (or girl) reaching out toward a goose as if to pet it, but at the very moment the picture was snapped it seemed the boy had just realized that the goose might bite him. So the boy's hand is frozen in space as the urge to pet the goose is exactly and proportionally balanced by the fear of being bitten by the goose if he tries to pet it and so he is stuck, frozen at an impasse as he cannot sense which way he *really* wants to move … toward or away from the goose."

    An extended metaphor is below of a different more complicated approach/avoidance problem such as concerning intimacy but masked by what appears to be a choice between options or an approach/approach problem.

    "I had the thought that if a duck was to come onto the scene, then the boy might become distracted and wonder which animal he wanted to pet and he would appear to be frozen or stuck between the two interesting birds, not sure which one he wanted to pet the most. But… of course, we would know that he was really afraid to pet either, although the little boy might forget all about that dilemma as it reminds him of very uncomfortable feelings."

2. The story of the "Strange Monkey Trap" illustrates being trapped by a desire and losing one's entire self to it. The story goes like this:

"In a certain region of the world, there is a species of monkey that can be trapped because it traps itself. Some goodies are put in a large, extremely heavy jar that has a very narrow neck. The monkey reaches into the jar to get the goodies, but once he is holding the goodies, his fist is too large to pass back out through the narrow neck. The only way the monkey can get free is to let go of the goodies, but he will not let go of the goodies and it appears he 'believes' or acts as if somehow he can get his freedom and keep the goodies too. When the trappers come by and the monkey sees them, he still holds fast to the goodies and he will not let go of the goodies even to run from the trappers and so he is caught and sold. The monkey also behaves as if those particular goodies are essential and could not be replaced by others later."

3. "You know of the picture (show if possible) of the woman that can look like a very old woman or a young, beautiful woman. What you see depends on *how* you look at it. Some people see the old woman and some the young woman. But some people *can learn how to view* the picture *differently* and then they can *see things in a new* way."

4. "How could it be true that parallel lines meet in space as Albert Einstein has shown? Yet it is true. It is true that parallel lines do not and cannot meet ordinarily. But at some time and in some place they do meet. So what is true under one set of rules in one place and at one time may not be true at another time, under different rules, in another place. The rules may differ in different times and different places so that what works or seems to work at one time and place may not necessarily work or be the case at another time or place. The way things are or seem to be can change."

5. Characteristics of various animals often lend themselves to metaphor and story. "Once there was a porcupine who would fire off his needles whenever he got angry. Besides getting a lot of needles shot back at him by other porcupines, he would also accidentally shoot his own needles at himself and this made him hurt even worse." Metaphors are best when they relate to the theme of the problem as well as to the interests of the person, who can then find possible solutions to the dilemma staying within the metaphor.

Metaphors Can Imply a Solution

6. The "Early Learning Set" (modified and adapted from Erickson, Rossi, and Rossi, 1976, p. 6 ff.) is vintage but still golden.

    "Now I want to talk to you ... If you like you may close your eyes and listen, or focus on something else in the room or you may look at me or you may look around as you please (covers all possibilities)."

    "When you first went to school the matter of learning the letters of the alphabet and the numbers may have seemed like a big insurmountable task. To recognize a small letter "a" and to distinguish a capital letter "O" from a capital "Q" can seem very difficult. And then too, longhand and print seemed so different. But you learned to form a mental image of some kind. At the time you did not know it but it was a permanent mental image. And later on in grammar school you formed other mental images of words or pictures of sentences."

    "You developed more and more mental images without knowing you were developing mental images. And you can recall all those images so that now you can form your letters almost automatically. The image and the memory of how to form it are tucked away and can be used almost automatically and effortlessly *you have learned them so well.*" (The implied message is that we have learned much and that we can still learn, though it may seem hard at first.)

7. "Sometimes *the best way to get a car out of a ditch* is by rocking it: first going forward and then backward, back and forth, back and forth and finally with the momentum of the rocking, it comes out of the ditch. Maybe going forward, maybe in reverse. By then there is so much mud, does it really matter? So, it may be that *sometimes cleaning up afterwards is the only way out*. Then again, often it works neatly and with ease."

© J.E. Talley, Ph.D.

16.

Therapeutic Stories and Tales

Therapeutic stories and tales should arouse, fix and hold interest by way of identification. The therapist must be attuned to waning or building interest. Thus, the themes of the central character should be very similar to, if not the same as, the themes and conflicts (wishes, fears, and maybe coping styles, defenses, and/or symptoms) of the patient, client, or seeker. Therefore, the main character may also have the same or a similar problem(s) and the same or similar means of coping. But something has to happen to change things so that the problem is dealt with "differently" or the problem becomes less of a problem by a change in how it is interpreted or seen. Interest in the tale is also held by means of suspense and curiosity as to the outcome and its means.

Fairy tales are the classics in part because we all (at times, or as children, or in dreams) feel like a prince or princess at home in the castle with the king and queen or we may feel more like an adopted stepchild like Cinderella. Stories about children move the listener back to childhood in a way and this enhances the possibility of re-working things. Good metaphors for accessing the unconscious or out of awareness processes are walks in the forest, going across or into the ocean, into a cave, visits with and dialogues with archetypal figures such as a fairy godmother, a wise old man or other benign helpful figure who will say or do something "important, helpful, useful, or hopeful."

Often multiple possible outcomes leave many solution options to the problem open. The specific outcome may be left unspoken or left the same except to note greater mastery as in the "swimmer felt much, much better since even though the waves stayed high, she noticed that she was becoming a stronger and more skillful swimmer." Multiple outcomes may be offered by addendum to a tale. For example, "But her twin sister on the other hand..." or "Nevertheless, other princesses from that very same kingdom found a different pathway through the forest and to the lake."

The exact means of the transformation is perhaps best left unspecified to allow the listener to generate the most relevant one for them from their own unconscious, *but* the methods can be stated. The therapist may say that the listener got a symbol, had a dream or met "someone" who prompted "a thought" or "some words" (unspecified) that in turn allowed the listener to become *aware* of: (1) things in a *new* way; (2) old things seemingly forgotten; and/or (3) unrecognized inner parts and resources that were helpful in letting go of something that is: (a) a loss of sorts, but with the freedom and excitement and happiness of going on to something new or better for this time and place for the seeker; (b) accepting something with greater mastery; and/or (c) making something at least somewhat different. Often a significant part of what needs to be reckoned with at the root is a belief about the self, others or the world that is intertwined with an attachment to someone.

1. The Little Girl Who Did Not Want To Turn Five

Once there was a little girl who, the night before her fifth birthday, began to cry and call for her mother. The little girl told her mother, "I've changed my mind. I don't want to turn five. I really don't want to start kindergarten. I want to keep on doing what I'm doing now longer." The little girl would hear nothing at all good about turning five so finally her mother posed a *different possibility* since it was agreed that tomorrow would come and the little girl would have to be something different than four. Her mother asked her if she would be willing to be just four plus three hundred and sixty-six days. The little girl agreed with relief. Several weeks later, it seemed that the little girl was finding it too tiresome to tell everyone she was four plus three hundred and some days and the little girl said, "Mommy, I'm tired of this long age. I think I should just be five now," and her mother agreed.

2. The Boy Who Had A Heart Attack When He Began College… (Almost)

Once there was a very nice young man who was loved dearly by his parents and he loved them dearly too. When he left home to go to college, he missed greatly playing baseball as he had been very good at it in high school, but now in college so many others were better at baseball that he would not get to play on the team. About a week later, soon after a visit from his parents had ended, his heart started to thump loudly and quickly, very loudly and very quickly until the boy thought he was going to have a heart attack. So he went to the hospital emergency room and was eventually told that he was not having a heart attack.

The next day he talked with a middle-aged man and the boy told him what had happened with his heart. The man asked about what had happened to him before his heart trouble and how he missed baseball and so forth about how good things had been at home. The man asked the boy how he had felt beginning kindergarten or daycare before going to school and the boy said he could not recall, but had been told that he had become sick upon beginning daycare. The middle-aged man agreed with the boy that leaving home to go to daycare for the first time could be so frightening that it could make one sick. The middle-aged man then told the boy the story of the little girl who did not want to turn five. He also told the boy it was true that life could seem much scarier now with all that college meant concerning having to really get ready for life in a new way and become (on some unspecified date)... a grown man. The boy was also told a story about another boy who had heart trouble of this type when he was about to become a young man and that this boy had feared he would die of a heart attack. The middle-aged man noted that when this other boy told his heart, after learning he had no medical problems, that he would not let this type of heart pounding make him do or not do anything that would keep him from growing into a young man *even if* he *died* in the process. His heart then stopped bothering him.

3. The Little Girl Who Knew the Sky Was Purple

Once there was a little girl whose mother seemed to believe that the sky was purple. Her mother would always refer to the sky as purple and would act very hurt and sad or even angry if the little girl ever said the sky was blue. So the little girl learned very well that she must always say that the sky was purple because if she did not, her mother would become very upset and when the mother was upset she did not take good care of the little girl and the little girl somehow understood this. Finally, the little girl decided in the back, underside of her mind, that life would be much easier if she would just actually see the sky as purple and believe it to be purple since she had to live with her mother and depended on her mother. This seemed to be a great improvement as the little girl no longer tried to convince her mother that the sky was really blue and neither did the little girl feel guilty for deceiving her mother. Then one day the little girl began to go to school and all the children thought that the sky was blue and so the little girl began to try to convince them whenever she could that the sky was really purple and that she knew this to be so.

4. The Little Girl Who Cut Herself Down With Sharp Words (and Sometimes Razor Blades)

Once there was a very nice little girl who like all little children — even very nice ones — would every now and then do something that displeased her father. Her father was very, very hard to always please and when he was angry with her, he would take her into a dark closet and there he would mercilessly scold her and berate her with cutting insults and pinch her. When the little girl would begin to cry, he would then tell her how much he really loved her even though he had just hurt her badly. When the little girl grew into a young woman and married, she would often have arguments with her husband for she married someone who was also very critical and difficult to please. After these arguments, she would go into a dark closet and berate herself with cutting, self-critical thoughts. Often she would speak them out loud and when she would finally burst into tears she would suddenly feel that she could love herself again. But sometimes she had to pinch herself and then finally cut herself with a razor blade before she could feel loveable again. The young woman at times said she inflicted this pain on herself to release tension and to feel as if she was alive. Of course, before cutting herself and criticizing herself, she was lost in despair and did not feel alive at all.

5. Implied solution:

One day the little boy who wanted to pet the goose but was afraid of being bitten (see section on metaphors of the problem) was taken on a trip by his grandfather to a zoo where there were many animals and one of them was a giant goose that the little boy's grandfather told him was— an ostrich. It had oh, such large eyes and it was oh, so very huge and towering and its beak was horribly big! The little boy was frightened by it. The longer he stared at the giant goose the more fascinated he became. Finally, he fed the giant goose and he did so again and again until the ostrich bit him. *But* although he was frightened and cried at first, he soon realized that he was more frightened than hurt and that the bite was really a pinch because the bird had no teeth. When the grandfather brought the boy home, he ran immediately to the goose and petted it. After all, he had survived a bite from a giant goose so what could hurt him here? Perhaps he would've pet the goose even if he had only just fed the ostrich since now the goose seemed so much smaller. (A story for use in tandem with the earlier stories in the last section of encountering a goose and a goose with a duck and especially with people who have anxiety related to intimacy among other things.)

6. Implied solution:

In order for the monkey grasping the goodies in the jar (see the last section) not to have been caught, he probably would have had to see some other way that he could get those or better goodies in a way that was more under his *own* control since he was a younger monkey and could not bear the thought of just leaving the goodies behind. He might have been shown a nearby goodie tree that had goodies with seeds in them so that he could plant them and grow his own goodies. Perhaps he could be intrigued into considering other possibilities by another monkey who would ask him questions like, "How much popcorn do you think you'll have to eat before you are no longer thirsty?" (A story for those who seem unable to act on what they "know.")

© J.E. Talley, Ph.D.

17.

Opposite Feeling Affect Bridge Variation

Simply ask for a vivid description of the problematic emotional state and then ask:

1. "What is the *opposite* of that problem feeling for you?

2. Please *describe* that *vividly* for me.

3. If you wish, let yourself *get comfortable and close your eyes,* (pause)

4. *Recall* a time in your life when you had a feeling that is the opposite of the problem feeling. Just nod when you have it so that I'll know, but take your time.

5. Now imagine that your life is on video. Go to a frame of that moment *and see yourself experiencing that opposite feeling* at some time in your life...

6. *Feel those feelings* and those physical bodily sensations again now. Just nod... when you have it... so that I'll know.

7. What enabled you to feel that way then? (use pauses as needed.) Just nod when you have it.

8. What inner resource does it feel like you would need to activate this more positive feeling now, or more often, ...under your own control for the betterment and general well-being of your total

personality? (Repeat last phrase, which seems to be a good general suggestive phrase.) Just nod when you have it so that I'll know, but take your time...

9. Can you now recall another time when you felt that opposite feeling? Just nod when you have it, but take your time.

10. See it in *another frame in the video of your life...* Experience those feelings and bodily sensations now... (Repeat 7 and 8.)

11. *And let's do this one more time*, etc. (for a total of three episodes).

12. Now imagine all of the *frames condensing* and collapsing into one large ball of energy throbbing with that feeling and those bodily sensations.

13. *Take them inside of your chest* and experience the sensations of that feeling growing, pulsating, and throbbing with the energy of that feeling and sensation throughout your body *now*. Just nod when you've done that so that I'll know, but take your time...

14. Notice how rewarding it feels. You might *anchor that feeling to a signal or cue* like pinching yourself or blinking.

15. *Practice this* a couple of times a day as you work out in this emotional weight room!

16. And *open your* eyes, joining me again in the here and now, and tell me anything you'd like to talk about that happened."

© J.E. Talley, Ph.D.

18.

Some Contributions of Milton Erickson Regarding Therapeutic Communication

Erickson attempted to promote constructive change, adaptation, and mastery by prompting the person to see the problem and the context of the problem including the person's own inner resources from a different vantage point or perspective. This was to be done in a somewhat different state of consciousness, unencumbered or less encumbered by some of the limitations of the person's history. The temporary suspending of the usual "framework" by and through which the problem has been seen is used in order to consider a "reframing" of the problem. The reframing may then be followed by a different response to the situation or problem. This is accomplished through the following sequence:

1. Fixation of attention
2. Depotentiating conscious sets
3. Unconscious search
4. Unconscious processes
5. A new response

1. *The fixation of attention* may be done by anything that gets and then holds the other person's attention. Initially the therapist may get the person's attention by doing something unexpected such as responding in an intriguing way in word or action within tolerable limits. For example, the remark might be made to the appropriate

patient, client, or seeker, "Of course my questions may at times seem a little strange, but aren't psychotherapists all a bit strange?" The other person is somewhat surprised that the therapist makes such a self-observation at all, let alone aloud. A key point here in keeping attention focused on the therapist (when that is desired) is to avoid saying and doing things in the highly expected almost stereotypical therapist manner. To arouse curiosity and attention, the therapist may pick up a nearby object (e.g., a toy) and study it, or make comments about a plant in the office (e.g., "It's quite noticeable that plants always grow toward the light").

Another way to fix attention is to use imagery, stories, words, and metaphors that are highly meaningful to the person because of their interest in the item (e.g., plants), the activity (e.g., skiing) or a thematic similarity (e.g., a little porcupine who would feel angry at times and somewhat fearful, but when he tried to shoot his needles toward another somehow always hit himself). This technique first focuses the person's attention on the therapist out of surprise, but then it moves the focus of attention to the person's own interior as the theme is heard. Attention is then further directed to their own interior with the therapist's permissive directives such as, "If you'd like to, you may now let your body and mind feel more and more comfortable as you focus your attention inward. You can be aware of the sound of my voice or other things, but these are unimportant. What is important is that you under your own control become more and more aware of your body and how it feels as you allow it to feel more and more comfortable as you effortlessly just notice your thoughts and feelings." This then leads to step 2.

2. *Depotentiating conscious sets* might be defined loosely as jolting, jogging, melting, or intriguing the person out of their usual way of looking at things for moments or longer to let new learning, ideas, and possibilities occur in the mind and perhaps in behavior. The therapist might ask, for example, "How would you describe the color of that feeling?" And then, "How would you describe the odor of that feeling? and the taste of that feeling? (and) What shape would you say that feeling might be?" and finally saying very slowly, "The mind is very interesting. That which seems to be in the foreground at this moment, my voice, may recede into the background in the next moment and other sounds or thoughts may come to the foreground and my voice may recede into the background...my voice in the foreground other sounds in the background... (silent pause for a few seconds); other sounds in the foreground...my voice in the background... (silent pause for a few seconds) foreground... background... background... foreground... conscious... unconscious... unconscious... conscious. That which was pressing on this day two years ago is now less in the foreground and may even seem forgotten ...things change over time, foreground... background... background... foreground... conscious... unconscious... unconscious... conscious. 'Now there are many ways in which the mind can function in which the unconscious can join with the conscious... many different ways in which the unconscious

can join the conscious mind and many ways the unconscious mind can tell the conscious mind a secret, without the conscious mind knowing that it has just received a gift!' " (The last sentence is from Erickson, Rossi, and Rossi, 1976, p. 68). The therapist may repeat elements to deepen the ideas. This leads directly to step 3.

3. The *unconscious search* may begin with the daydream method, metaphors alluding to the problematic theme and implying several possible solutions often with multiple metaphors, or the use of stories and tales. Steps 4 and 5 occur internally at the individual's own rate and in accord with the needs of their whole personality.

4. With regard to *unconscious processes*, it is noted that the famous Zeigarnik Effect shows that in follow-up interviews assessing recall of a number of tasks in the lab, experimental subjects were more likely to recall non-completed tasks than completed tasks.

5. When *a new response,* step 5, is achieved and is either behavioral and overt or is cognitive or emotional and covert as in a new way(s) of thinking and/or feeling about things; the response may be experienced by the person as spontaneous or "happening all by itself". Thus, seemingly minimizing the effects of treatment. The brief therapist must be prepared to let the person keep this perspective as it validates their potential, capacity, and autonomy.

Finally, Erickson's use of permissive language must be emphasized (e.g., "You may begin to… You might notice… Is it possible that… etc.") as well as his use of giving little to resist or fight with while expressing certainty that something will happen though he does not know what or when. He attempts to get his patients to "become curious" about this and "wonder when it might *begin* to change" and consider some possibilities regarding what could happen to make things "different".

19.

Micro-Technique of the Problem Solving Daydream and Active Imagination

This micro-technique is designed to utilize the person's "creative unconscious" as a repository of meanings, solutions, and next steps as did Carl Jung, Milton Erickson, and others. The therapist makes references to "the back burner of the mind, the underside of the mind", or the conscious and unconscious and states something like the following modified and adapted from the collected works of Milton Erickson (Rossi, 1980):

1. "Your unconscious has its own way of looking at things and when you dream your unconscious mind has a very creative way of showing you things... ways of seeing or looking at things and feeling about things that may be very different from the usual and ordinary ways of seeing things when you are awake. Likewise, while driving the car you may have a thought come to mind that offers a new possibility... something different. Your unconscious mind can be very creative, so in a moment I would like to ask you about the possibility of using it. (This creates a sense of expectancy, curiosity, and attentiveness. All of this is often a good "set up" for the following, which also may be said by itself.)

2. How about if you take a moment now and if it feels comfortable enough, allow yourself to close your eyes as you let yourself feel even more comfortable, just more and more comfortable.

3. I want to ask your unconscious mind about the possibility of you having a daydream — not a fantasy that you consciously or intentionally guide — but a daydream that unfolds the way *it seems to wish to* unfold while you *simply receive it* or see, hear, or experience it so that something could happen that you would *not expect* to happen… so that something could happen that might even *surprise* you. You may have words come to mind, see an image or have a set of images — anything at all will do — a picture, a voice of your innermost self or of some figure… just take whatever comes up as long as it is helpful, feels positive and is somehow related to giving you a resolution or a good next step to your dilemma. It may be an inner resource that we need to activate or free-up or the opposite counter-balancing feeling you need to activate to manage more effectively in order to *gain some mastery*. And since it is your unconscious we want to hear from, let's let it answer in a different way.

4. How about if you allow the unconscious to communicate with your fingers? Let your right index finger raise for 'yes,' the left index finger for 'no,' and the right thumb can raise for 'maybe,' 'I don't know,' or 'I don't wish to answer yet.' (Fingers can be reversed for left-handed people.) Just let it happen to a finger while you simply observe with curiosity which finger will move

as if it were happening to you without any effort or conscious intention on your part.

5. The question I would like to ask your unconscious mind is…, 'Is it in the best interest of your personality as a whole for your unconscious mind to give your conscious mind a gift, such as a daydream like the one I described, related to a solution or good next step for the problem that you want help with?'

6. There are many ways the unconscious mind and the conscious mind can communicate…many ways in which the unconscious mind can share a secret with the conscious mind without the conscious mind ever realizing that it has just received a gift.

7. Now I'm going to count to three and when I say 'three' let's see which finger moves effortlessly, automatically, and seemingly under its own control. One…becoming curious…what will happen? Two… effortlessly, automatically, and seemingly under its own control. Right index finger raised means 'yes,' the left index finger raised means 'no,' and the right thumb raised for 'maybe,' 'I don't know,' or 'I don't wish to answer'. Three…

8. Is it in the best interest of your personality as a whole for you to have a daydream like the one described to be of help to you with this current problem? Be curious and observe which finger will move? (Wait. If there is a "yes" response, proceed. Any other response can be used as ambivalence to explore with or without

daydreams. Whatever the response, when any finger lifts say, "Very Good" to reinforce that degree of use of the unconscious.)

9. Go ahead now and let the daydream begin when I say 'three' if it hasn't already begun... One... curious about what will come to mind... Two... effortlessly, spontaneously, and seemingly under its own control... *My* conscious mind does not know what will emerge neither does my unconscious mind know. *Your* conscious mind may not know either, but your unconscious mind can wonder and come to some understanding of what I will ask. Three... dream... and just nod whenever you're through so that I'll know, but take the time you need. (After the nod, continue.)

10. Very Good. I don't know when or how this resource will become active for you... tomorrow... the next day... tonight or... in a month and you may not know precisely when it began, but you can trust in this new found resource inside of you and be hopeful about its possibilities.

11. And open your eyes, joining me again in the here and now, and tell me anything you'd like to talk about that happened."

© J.E. Talley, Ph.D.

20.

Active Imagination and the Inner Guide

This exercise has its origins in the Native American ritual of the totem animal dream such as the one attributed to Sitting Bull before the Battle of Little Big Horn and the active imagination work of Carl Jung (Chodorow, 1997). This adaptation is based on the work of Martin Rossman (2000).

IN PREPARATION

Rule out those with psychotic symptoms, delusional people and those with whom you would not use insight-oriented treatments.

With careful use, it can be quite helpful with dissociative patients, those with PTSD and abuse victims. However, care is needed so as not to re-traumatize them with non-wise, non-compassionate stimuli.

To yourself *note* how they respond to the guide. This is indicative of transference themes and facilitates reframing, constructive de-identification, and looking at things through the eyes of wisdom and love instead of the eyes of aloneness and fear.

INSTRUCTIONS

This is a dialogue with an inner figure who has: 1) Wisdom, 2) Compassion, and 3) No strings attached concerning the specifics of what you do about the problem.

Give yourself permission to stop at any time or not to do this if you are feeling fragile or uncomfortable with it.

Allow yourself to get comfortable and whenever you are ready close your eyes.

In the mind's eye, pick a safe, comfortable place and be there now. Just nod when you are done to let me know, but take your time.

Go to the safest spot in the safe, comfortable place. Notice the colors, sounds, and odors of this safe, comfortable place, and just nod again when you've done this so that I'll know, but take your time.

Invite an image to form or to come onto the scene of a being of any type or kind that is real, a fantasy, an animal, or a person. It could be from literature, from the past, or from the present, or it could be a spiritual being like Buddha or Jesus, or it could be a cartoon figure like Bugs Bunny, but... when you feel ready, invite the guide to become clearer and clearer, welcome the image, carefully observe it, notice its qualities. If it does not seem *BOTH WISE AND KNOWING, AND KIND AND LOVING*, send it away. (Have person nod, etc., when done.)

Ask it by what name you should call it so it can be accessed anytime and anywhere. (You now have the most available and affordable co-therapist ever.) You may touch the figure if that seems appropriate.

Begin to focus on the question you would like to ask about the problem or dilemma that you have and let it begin to form in your mind. If possible, form the question in a solution-oriented, possible-to-accomplish, focused way.

When you are ready, ask it the question you have come to ask.

Allow your Inner Guide to share its wisdom with you and its compassion for you. Nod whenever you are finished to let me know, but take your time. Carefully consider its responses. (long pause)

If you would like to ask questions to understand its responses, go ahead and carry on a dialogue for as long as you like to get what you need now. Nod whenever you are finished so that I will know, but take your time.

Imagine for a few moments that you act on its guidance. Who would be involved? What obstacles might come up? Just notice these without judging them. (long pause)

See how you might deal with these obstacles in a constructive way. (long pause)

Notice if you have learned anything. (long pause)

Is there anything you want to remember before you come back to the outer world? (long pause)

Ask the guide to tell you the surest and best way to reconnect with it in the future.

Thank it, if that seems appropriate, say your farewell and allow the image to fade. Just nod when you are finished so that I will know, but take your time.

Open your eyes when you are ready and take about 5 minutes now to write or draw about your experience even if you feel not much happened.

Did anything happen that you want to talk with me about?

© J.E. Talley, Ph.D.

21.

Contrasting Videos: A Variation of the Miracle Question

This is a version of the Miracle Question initially recognized by Insoo Kim Berg as a powerful intervention. The first description of its usefulness was published by her colleague and founder of solution focused brief therapy (SFBT), Steve de Shazer (1988, p. 5). The re-phrasing below is to adapt it to a contrasting videos variation.

For this exercise, the therapist needs to speak slowly and clearly and using future-directed words at the beginning of this solution-building process. The answer to the first question is an opener that needs to be explored and developed. Be sure to use "when", "would", or "will" and not "if". The therapist speaks as below:

"Now, I want to ask you a strange question. Suppose that, the problem which brought you here is now solved. If I were to look at a video of the situation with the problem solved—how would it look different than the video of the problem? So, what will look different when this change occurs, that will tell you that a change has happened, and the problem which brought you here is now solved?" (Expectant pause)

"So, when would you say was the last time a part of this difference or change happened, even a little bit?"

"Tell me about that. What might a hidden camera video show that you did to influence a little bit of the change that day?"

"So, what would it take for you to continue to do what you started that day?"

"What would the hidden camera video show that others close to you would say it would take for you to repeat this?"

"What is the first small step that we can visualize you taking to make a little bit of it happen?"

"That sounds like a big step. What step might have to come beforehand that is smaller and that we can visualize you doing right away if you really choose to?"

"Now, imagine that the change has happened, (describe), what would our video camera show that you will be doing that you are not doing right now?" or "What will you be doing instead of X?"

"And when you are doing that (something different and positive that the change allows), what will the hidden camera video show that others who are important to you will do in response to this?"

"What will they be doing that is different?"… and "How will that make a difference to you?"…and, "How will they describe you then?"

If the client's response is to describe inner emotions, ask them to describe the visible actions a video would show once they have these feelings by saying, "Suppose you find this _____ (emotion/ feeling) tomorrow after the change, what do you suppose that a video would show is different about you that will let you know that you now have this _____ (inner feeling)?"

If the client can't do this exercise then ask, "What is there that suggests that the problem can be solved?"

© J.E. Talley, Ph.D.

22.

Therapist Wordings of Comments and Responses

(Numbers 1-4 below are in Milton Erickson style and 5-10 are in a more process focused or cognitive style.)

Comments should be as gentle and permissive as possible initially. (For example, "Is it possible that _____?"), but may escalate to stating something like, "It's my sense that _____," as appears useful. (Here I favor the Strupp and Binder and M. Erickson styles and have not found the styles of Sifneos, Malan, Davanloo or at times Mann to be as effective).

1. "Is it fair to say that at times, for example, when we talk about _____, when I ask you about _____, or at times when you think about _____ (for example, asking her on a date, telling him you don't want to go, asking for something…) that you feel at least somewhat uncomfortable?" This assumes the therapist needs to start at a very low threat level. Then the therapist can "nickel and dime it" upward (for example to using, "Perhaps you feel even *quite* uncomfortable?" and "*most* of the time?" With an affirmation here the therapist can go on to something like, "When you feel uncomfortable like that do you have the sense that you do something, maybe just in your mind, to avoid that discomfort?"

2. "Is it possible that you keep feelings about (for example, his death, your divorce, losing your job) tucked away in a separate

compartment ('the lower drawer or a back filing cabinet') of your mind?"

3. "I noticed that your eyelids closed for a split second and you looked tired suddenly when I asked you about this, a bit like you did last week (or two weeks ago, or a few minutes ago). What do you imagine that tiredness might be about?" If the response is, "nothing," or "I need some sleep," then the therapist might follow up with, "I wonder if *another part* of your mind can *begin* to consider the *possibility* that while what you say is true, there may be some other important thoughts or feelings related to your tiredness and I wonder if *that part* of your mind could assume this possibility and tell me *if* some other feelings *were to be there*, what might they be?"

4. Rather than saying, "It seems that when I ask you about your mother you often bring the focus rather quickly back to your father," the more Ericksonian therapist would usually not be so direct in this way, but would rather perhaps attempt to absorb the person's attention deeply by getting in sync with body posture, breathing, language, eye blinks, etc. and then attempt to shift the state of mind and say something like, "and of course, you must not tell me the things we shouldn't know about your mother until you are really ready to do so and I have no idea when that will be. It might come forth today, next week, a year from now or, perhaps it has already begun to be ready to be told, I really don't know."

5. "Is it possible that some of the things that ____ (e.g., irritate, annoy, or anger) you about others, are traits that are important to you in some way with regard to yourself?"

6. "It seems like there's not much feeling associated with ____ (e.g., her death). If you were to hear another person speak of ____ (e.g., such a death) what feelings might you expect to be there?"

7. "Is there any possibility you have some feelings of frustration with ____ (e.g., your husband 'helping out' in these ways that end up constraining you)?"

   – Anything that serves to move one away from the emotions and thoughts associated with parts of the focus, may be a protective coping method to manage it as well as a method of avoidance. The method of avoidance might be brought into the focus as a method of coping, not forgetting that we all need defenses and that it is possible to permit a new perspective by melting, perforating, getting around their radar, or by transforming (beginning to transform) the coping mechanisms toward something more adaptive such as creative expression.

8. Good work with intense intellectualization can often occur by reference to truthful paradoxes that are at first confusing. For example, the unreasonability of pure reason, that parallel lines

meet in space, that ultimately the desire to be in control may take control.

9. For work with those who have not had a psychotic episode, are less fragile, and have some traits frequently described as "narcissistic" or "borderline" and especially for people prone to see themselves as "all bad", it may be useful to first teach them some self-soothing techniques utilizing positive imagery and physical comfort including some linkage via imagery with a "good self-part" to use as needed. The insight work would still be around a Core Conflictual Relationship Theme (CCRT), but coupled with a focus on their cognitive-style such that it might become a more effective coping mechanism.

Thus, more "narcissistic" (self-esteem sensitive) people can be helped by relating their CCRT to the inner pattern of idealization and devaluation (e.g., "When you first met her it sounded like you wondered if you were good enough for her. Now it seems you're seeing her in a different light. She's off the pedestal and you're wondering if she's good enough or adequate enough in some ways for you.")

From the detailed history of similar prior relationships it can be gleaned whether this is a repetitive pattern. If so, then it might be asked, "Do you think you tend to put, new potential romantic partners (or people in general or bosses) on somewhat of a pedestal and think that things are going to be wonderful with them? ...Would it be fair to say that you may idealize them?"

"Would it be fair to say that this seems to be more likely to happen when you are feeling more critical or down on yourself? Then, later on when for some reason when you become disappointed in them or irritated with them, things switch. The other person is then seen or felt to be "not so great after all," "just like all the rest," "mediocre," or "boring" as you begin to see yourself as not so bad after all and a good guy with some "unique" or "special" qualities." Once the shortcomings of another have been identified, the therapist can then explore whether the person tends to devalue the formerly idealized other person. A boost to this interpretation occurs when the therapist can elicit thoughts about the idealization/devaluation process with the therapist.

Note the absence of simply trying to interpret the perception of the therapist's shortcomings as transferential and having little or no basis in reality. The perceptions are either owned or at least not dismissed and then the therapist empathizes with the person's disappointment in the therapist. This can be beneficial in learning that others do not always feel the need to cast themselves as perfect and can still accept and even feel good about themselves and therefore, so might they. Here the therapist has hopefully shown sufficient lack of self-esteem concerns or "injury" so that the person can internalize the response and gradually become less concerned with perfection, beauty, potency, wealth, or intelligence with regard to self and others while catching the idealization/devaluation pattern and style. A second step may be the clarification of the typical responses when others disappoint or criticize. That may be the response of withdrawal or rage (fast flight or flaming fury).

10. With those who engage in "all good/all bad" feelings, but who are non-suicidal, have low fragmentation, no history of a psychotic episode, and show potential after developing self-soothing capacities and techniques, the therapist might venture to help to clarify the tendency to see things as "all good" or "all bad" (splitting). The therapist can note that it is "very understandable" to feel such admiration or such anger when one is relating to only half or part of the picture. For example, it might be said, "As you describe this, it sounds like your apartment mate is pretty bad, almost "completely bad" and when you talk about your new friend she sounds so good, almost "completely good." After some affirmations of such feeling states the therapist might ask, "Is it fair to say that you often experience things or people at least for brief moments or short periods of time as pretty much all one way or the other, such as strong or weak, friendly or unfriendly?" The therapist could also inquire, "Do you find it hard to carry one set of feelings from one situation forward in time so that new, perhaps troublesome experiences with a person are seen together with earlier

satisfying experiences?" Finally, to begin a change in the person's perception, the therapist might say, "What would it be like for you to experiment with doing some self-soothing as we've done before while you imagine in your mind's eye a picture of 'good Mary' mixing with a picture of 'bad Mary' to form one whole person who's different as a whole than either part." This is done after eliciting detail and images associated with the two conflicting parts. This work, if undertaken, seems best done with great care and constant attention for the other person's state and emphasizing there are "understandable" reasons things are experienced this way so that self-blame is avoided.

© J.E. Talley, Ph.D.

23.

Thoughts on the Brief Treatment of Grief

1. Is the deceased idealized or vilified such that only either the "good" or "bad" aspects of the deceased are reacted to and felt? If so, key work is probably in the area of evoking the opposite split-off image. This may require more therapist activity than usual. Neither gods nor devils die. Some more normal level of "splitting" may be operative. Can the person say what they liked very much and what they disliked about the deceased and have the corresponding emotion during the same few minutes? Activating the emotions that are the opposite of what is usually conscious may do much to facilitate the grieving process. If this "splitting" isn't addressed, a split off "all good" or "all bad" image may be hidden and activated only at certain times, preventing acceptance of the loss.

2. Asking the person what they wish they could have said to the deceased or heard the deceased say to them before death may provide key material. This material may become emotionally alive in the hour by using the Gestalt technique (carefully so that affect is titrated) of "talking to the empty chair." The therapist asks the person to imagine the deceased is sitting in an office chair arranged to face them two or three feet away and then the person is asked to say whatever they wish could have been said to the deceased before their death. The person is also asked what

they wish they could have heard the deceased say to them. This is a dialogue and may go back and forth for some time and can be done on multiple occasions. If this method feels uncomfortable, something similar can be done by suggesting that the person write the deceased a letter expressing and asking about whatever was left unspoken. The deceased might be addressed in the language the two usually spoke in and addressed using the same familiar or personal form of address used in life and in their native language even if the therapist doesn't understand it. There can be time for translation later if necessary.

3. It might be asked if the person has visited the place where the deceased's remains are buried or ashes are scattered and suggested that they do so to facilitate the grieving process. They might also be asked if they feel almost as if they could round a corner and suddenly see the deceased there. Responses to these may indicate if the death has been emotionally accepted.

4. A bit more can be made of termination in grief work by setting a definite date for the work to end and counting down the sessions toward the end. If the person has had multiple losses or for other reasons seems unable to do well with yet another loss (of the therapist), then the termination can be simply left as, "I'm here and the door's open if you wish to contact me." However, if the approach taken is to reactivate the remaining grief for more final mastery at termination, then saying something like, "Now that

you've shared so many of your thoughts and feelings with me about (e.g., your brother), in a way, I've become a repository of your feelings about him so that saying good-bye to me may be a bit like saying good-bye to him all over again." This often evokes remaining grief.

© J.E. Talley, Ph.D.

24.

Closing and Ending in Brief Therapy

Outline of Considerations

Diagnostic Considerations

- Grief (significant losses in person's life; e.g., divorce in family, death, end of love relationship). Look for the reactivation of grief from childhood.

- Dependent and/or fragile character. Conflict centered around separation/ individuation may get activated.

Issues to Look For

- Feelings of loss (including sadness, anger, guilt)

- Will I make it without therapist?

- Frustration re: unmet goals of therapy

- Reactivation of initial symptoms

- Rekindling of previous losses

- Appreciation for work well done

Factors Leading to Good Closing

- Proper preparation - person notified well in advance and given opportunity to express feelings (disappointment, sadness, anger, affection/love)

- Well integrated ego (reasonably independent and supportive social network)

- Seen very briefly (less than 4 sessions)

- When goal(s) have been met

- A therapist who is comfortable with taking leave

- Keep discussion about termination within the boundaries of themes from the work, nature of the relationship, and goals of therapy.

Other Closing Tasks

- Future contacts/therapy. Conditions for re-entering therapy.
- Relationship with therapist in future (visits, letters).
- "After-work"
- Essential to make every effort to end on a positive note.

(Pinkerton & Rockwell, 1990)

References

Aguilera, D., & Messick, J. (1978). *Crisis intervention.* St. Louis, MO: Mosby.

Bauer, G., & Kobos, J. (1993). *Brief therapy: Short-term psychodynamic intervention.* Northvale, NJ: Jason Aronson, Inc.

Bennett, D., & Parry, G. (2004). Maintaining the therapeutic alliance: Resolving alliance threatening interactions related to the transference. In D. Charmin (Ed.), *Core processes in brief dynamic psychotherapy* (pp. 251-272). Mahwah, NJ: Lawrence Erlbaum Associates, Publishers.

Beutler, L. (2000). David and Goliath: When empirical and clinical standards of practice meet. *American Psychologist, 55* (9), 997-1007.

Binder, J. (2004). *Key competencies in brief dynamic psychotherapy.* New York, NY: Guilford Press.

Chodorow, J. (1997). *Jung on active imagination.* Princeton, NJ: Princeton University Press.

Connolly, M., Crits-Christoph, P., Shappell, S., Barber, J., Luborsky, L., & Shaffer, C. (1999). Relation of transference interpretations to outcome in the early sessions of brief supportive-expressive psychotherapy. *Psychotherapy Research, 9,* 485-495.

Crits-Christoph, P., Cooper, A., & Luborsky, L. (1988). The accuracy of therapists' interpretations and the outcome of dynamic psychotherapy. *Journal of Consulting and Clinical Psychology, 56,* 490-495.

Crits-Christoph, P., & Gibbons, M. (2002). Relational interpretations. In J. Norcross (Ed.), *Psychotherapy relationships that work* (pp. 285-300). New York, NY: Oxford University Press.

Davanloo, H. (1978). *Basic principles and techniques in short-term dynamic psychotherapy.* New York, NY: Spectrum Publishers.

de Shazer, S. (1988). *Clues: Investigating solutions in brief therapy.* New York, NY: W.W. Norton.

Eells, T., & Lombart, K. (2004). Case formulation: Determining the focus in brief dynamic psychotherapy. In D. Charmin (Ed.), *Core processes in brief dynamic psychotherapy* (pp. 119-143). Mahwah, NJ: Lawrence Erlbaum Associates, Publishers.

Elkin, I., Shea, M., Watkins, J., Imber, S., Sotsky, S., Collins, J., Glass, D., Pilkonis, P., Leber, W., Docherty, J., Fiester, S., & Parloff, M. (1989). National Institute of Mental Health treatment of depression collaborative research program: General effectiveness of treatments. *Archives of General Psychiatry, 46,* 971-982.

Erickson, M., Rossi, E., & Rossi, S. (1976). *Hypnotic realities*: The induction of clinical hypnosis and forms of indirect suggestion. New York, NY: Irvington Publishers, Inc.

Garfield, S. (1994). Research on client variables in psychotherapy. In A. Bergin & S. Garfield (Eds.), *Handbook of psychotherapy and behavior change* (4th ed., pp. 190-228). New York, NY: John Wiley & Sons.

Gibbons, M., Crits-Christoph, P., & Apostol, P. (2004). Constructing interpretations and assessing their accuracy. In D. Charmin (Ed.), *Core Processes in brief dynamic psychotherapy* (pp. 145-163). Mahwah, NJ: Lawrence Erlbaum Associates, Publishers.

Høgland, P. (1993). Transference and long-term change after dynamic psychotherapy of brief to moderate length. *American Journal of Psychotherapy, 47,* 494-507.

Høgland, P., & Piper, N. (1995). Focal adherence in brief dynamic psychotherapy: A comparison of findings from two independent studies. *Psychotherapy, 32,* 618-628.

Høgland, P., Sorlie, T., Heyerdahl, O., Sorbye, O., & Amlo, S. (1993). Brief dynamic psychotherapy: Patient suitability, treatment length and outcome. *Journal of Psychotherapy Practice and Research, 2,* 230-241.

Horowitz, M., Marmor, C., Weiss, D., Dewitt, K., & Rosenbaum, R. (1984). Brief psychotherapy of bereavement reactions: The relationship of process to outcome. *Archives of General Psychiatry, 41,* 438-448.

Horowitz, M., Marmor, C., Krupnick, J.,Wilner, N., Kaltreider, N., & Wallerstein, R. (1984). *Personality styles and brief psychotherapy.* New York, NY: Basic Books.

Horvath, A., & Bedi, R. (2002). The alliance. In J. Norcross (Ed.), *Psychotherapy relationships that work* (pp. 37-69). New York, NY: Oxford University Press.

Howard, K., Kopta, S., Krause, M., & Orlinsky, D. (1986). The dose-effect relationship in psychotherapy. *American Psychologist, 41,* 159-164.

Howard, K., Moras, K., Brill, P., Martinovich, Z., & Lutz, N. (1996). Evaluation of psychotherapy: Efficacy, effectiveness, and patient progress. *American Psychologist, 51,* 1059-1064.

Hubble, M., Duncan, B., & Miller, S. (1999). Introduction. In M. Hubble, B. Duncan, & S. Miller (Eds.), *The heart and soul of change*: What works in therapy (pp. 1-19). Washington, DC: American Psychological Association.

Joyce, A., & Piper, W. (1996). Dimensions and predictors of patient response to interpretations. *Psychiatry, 59,* 65-81.

Koss, M., & Shiang, J. (1994). Research on brief psychotherapy. In A. Bergin & S. Garfield (Eds.), *Handbook of psychotherapy and behavior change* (4th ed., pp. 1009-1016). New York, NY: John Wiley & Sons.

Lambert, M., & Anderson, E. (1996). Assessment for the time-limited psychotherapies. In L. Dickstein, M. Riba & J. Olvham (Eds.), *Review of psychiatry* (pp. 23-42). Washington, DC: American Psychiatric Press.

Lambert, M., & Barley, D. (2002). Research summary on the therapeutic relationship and psychotherapy outcome. In J. Norcross (Ed.), *Psychotherapy relationships that work* (pp. 17-32). New York, NY: Oxford University Press.

Lambert, M., Hunt, R., & Vermeersch, D. (2004). Optimizing outcome through prediction and measurement of psychological functioning. In D. Charmin (Ed.), *Core Processes in brief dynamic psychotherapy* (pp. 23-45). Mahwah, NJ: Lawrence Erlbaum Associates, Publishers.

Levenson, H. (2010). *Brief dynamic therapy*. Washington, DC: American Psychological Association.

Luborsky, L. (1984*). Principles of psychoanalytic psychotherapy: A manual for supportive-expressive treatment*. New York, NY: Basic Books.

Luborsky, L., & Crits-Christoph, P. (1990). *Understanding transference: The core conflictual relationship theme method.* New York, NY: Basic Books.

Luborsky, L., & Crits-Christoph, P. (2003). *Understanding transference: The core conflictual relationship theme method* (2nd ed.). Washington, DC: American Psychological Association.

Malan, D. (1976). *The frontier of brief psychotherapy*. New York, NY: Plenum Publishers.

Mann, J. (1973). *Time limited psychotherapy*. Cambridge, MA: Harvard University Press.

Marmor, J. (1979). Short-term dynamic psychotherapy. *The American Journal of Psychiatry, 136*, 149-155.

Najavits, L., & Strupp, H. (1994). Differences in the effectiveness of psychodynamic therapists: A process outcome study. *Psychotherapy, 31,* 114-123.

Norcross, J. (2002). Empirically supported therapy relationships. In J. Norcross (Ed.), *Psychotherapy relationships that work* (pp. 3-16). New York, NY: Oxford University Press.

Ogrodniczuk, J., Piper, W., Joyce, A., & McCallum, M. (1999). Transference interpretations in short-term dynamic psychotherapy. *Journal of Nervous and Mental Disease, 187,* 572-579.

Ogrodniczuk, J., & Piper, W. (2004). The evidence: Transference and patient outcomes - A comparison of types of patients. In D. Charman (Ed.), *Core processes in brief psychodynamic psychotherapy* (pp. 165-184). Mahwah, NJ: Lawrence Erlbaum Associates, Publishers.

Olfson, M., & Pincus, H. (1994). Outpatient psychotherapy in the United States, II: Patterns of utilization. *American Journal of Psychiatry, 15,* 1289-1294.

Pinkerton, R. (1986). Brief individual counseling and psychotherapy with students. In J. Talley & W. Rockwell (Eds.), *Counseling and psychotherapy with college students: A guide to treatment* (pp.1-30*).* New York, NY: Praeger Publishers.

Pinkerton, R., & Rockwell, W. (1990). Termination in brief psychotherapy: The case for an eclectic approach. *Psychotherapy, 27(3),* 362-365.

Pinkerton, R., Talley, J., & Cooper, S. (2009). Reflections on individual psychotherapy with university students: What seems to work. *Journal of College Student Psychotherapy, 23(3),* 153-183.

Piper, W. (1993). The use of transference interpretations. *American Journal of Psychotherapy, 47,* 477-478.

Piper,W., Joyce, A., McCallum, M., & Azim, H. (1993). Concentration and correspondence of transference interpretations in short-term psychotherapy. *Journal of Consulting and Clinical Psychology, 61,* 586-595.

Piper, W., Azim, H., Joyce, A., & McCallum, M. (1991). Transference interpretations, therapeutic alliance and outcome in short-term individual psychotherapy. *Archives of General Psychiatry, 48,* 946-953.

Rosen, S. (1982). *My voice will go with you: The teaching tales of Milton H. Erickson.* New York, NY: W.W. Norton and Company.

Rossi, E. (Ed.), (1980). *The collected papers of Milton H. Erickson on hypnosis.* New York, NY: Irvington Publishers, Inc.

Rossi, E., & Ryan M. (Eds.), (1992). *Creative choice in hypnosis: The seminars, workshops, and lectures of Milton H. Erickson.* New York, NY: Irvington Publishers, Inc.

Rossman, M. (2000). *Guided imagery for self-healing.* Novato, CA: H.J. Kramer.

Safran J. & Muran, J. (2000). *Negotiating the therapeutic alliance: A relational treatment guide.* New York, NY: Guilford Press.

Sanders, S. (1991*). Clinical self-hypnosis: The power of words and images.* New York, NY: Guilford Press.

Seligman, M. (1995). The effectiveness of psychotherapy: The Consumer Reports study. *American Psychologist, 50(12),* 965-974.

Shedler, J. (2010). The efficacy of psychodynamic psychotherapy. *The American Psychologist, 65(2),* 98-109.

Sifneos, P. (1979). *Short-term dynamic psychotherapy: Evaluation and technique.* New York, NY: Plenum Publishers.

Smith, M., Glass, G., & Miller, T. (1980). *The benefits of psychotherapy.* Baltimore, MD: Johns Hopkins University Press.

Strupp, H. & Binder, J. (1984). *Psychotherapy in a new key.* New York, NY: Basic Books.

Talley, J. (1992). Epilogue: Toward a model for very brief psychotherapy. In J. Talley, *The predictors of successful very brief psychotherapy: A study of differences by gender, age, and treatment variables* (pp. 138-143). Springfield, IL: Charles C. Thomas, Publisher.

Talley, J., Butcher, A., Maguire, M., & Pinkerton, R. (1992). The effects of very brief psychotherapy on symptoms of dysphoria. In J. Talley, *The predictors of successful very brief psychotherapy: A study of differences by gender, age, and treatment variables* (pp. 12-45). Springfield, IL: Charles C. Thomas, Publisher.

Talley, J., Butcher, A., & Moorman, J. (1992). Client satisfaction with very brief psychotherapy. In J. Talley, *The predictors of successful very brief psychotherapy: A study of differences by gender, age, and treatment variables* (pp. 46-84). Springfield, IL: Charles C. Thomas, Publisher.

Talley, J., & Clack, J. (2006). Use of the Outcome Questionnaire 45.2 with a university population. *Journal of College Student Psychotherapy, 20* (4), 5-15.

Talmon, M. (1990). Single session therapy: Maximizing the effect of the first (and often only) therapeutic encounter. New York, NY: John Wiley & Sons.

Wallas, L. (1985). *Stories for the third ear: Using hypnotic tales in psychotherapy.* New York, NY: W. W. Norton and Company.

Wampold, B. (2010). *The basics of psychotherapy.* Washington, DC: American Psychological Association.

Wampold, B. (2011). Psychotherapy is effective and here's why. As reported by A. Brown & K. Kelley. *Monitor on Psychology, 42(9),* 14.

Wampold, B., & Budge, S. (2012). The 2011 Leona Tyler Award Address: The relationship—and its relationship to the common and specific factors of psychotherapy. *The Counseling Psychologist, 40(4),* 601-623.

Watkins, J. (1971). The affect bridge: A hypnoanalytic technique. *International Journal of Clinical and Experimental Hypnosis, 19*(1), 21-27.

Winston, A., McCullough, L., & Laikin, M. (1993). Clinical and research implications of patient-therapist interaction in brief psychotherapy. *American Journal of Psychotherapy, 47,* 527-539.

Made in the USA
Charleston, SC
14 March 2014